P9-CKY-466

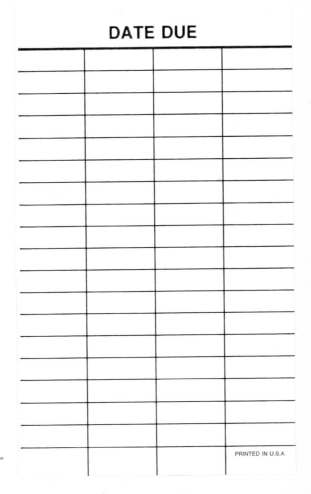

DATE DUE

CLIFFS NOTES

HARDBOUND   LITERARY   LIBRARIES

EUROPEAN LITERATURE LIBRARY

Volume 4

Scandinavian Literature

3 Titles

ISBN 0-931013-23-2

Library distributors, hardbound editions:
Moonbeam Publications
18530 Mack Avenue
Grosse Pointe, MI 48236
(313) 884-5255

MOONBEAM PUBLICATIONS
Robert R. Tyler, President
Elizabeth Jones, Index Editor

FOREWORD

Moonbeam Publications has organized **CLIFFS NOTES**, the best-selling popular (trade) literary reference series, into a fully indexed hardbound series designed to offer a more permanent format for the series.

Hardbound volumes are available in a **BASIC LIBRARY**, a 24 volume series. The current softbound series (over 200 booklets) has been divided into five major literary libraries to help researchers, librarians, teachers, students and all readers use this series more effectively. The five major literary groupings are further subdivided into 17 literary periods or genres to enhance the use of this series as a more precise literary reference book.

Hardbound volumes are also available in an **AUTHORS LIBRARY**, a 13 volume series classified by author, covering 11 authors and over 70 Cliffs Notes titles. This series helps readers who prefer to study the works of a particular author, rather than an entire literary period.

**CLIFFS NOTES HARDBOUND
LITERARY LIBRARIES**
1990 by
Moonbeam Publications
18530 Mack Avenue
Grosse Pointe, MI   48236
(313) 884-5255

Basic Library - 24 Volume
ISBN 0-931013-24-0

Authors Library - 13 Volume
ISBN 0-931013-65-8

Bound in U.S.A.

EUROPEAN LITERATURE LIBRARY

Volume 4

Scandinavian Literature

CONTENTS

Giants in the Earth

Ibsen's Plays I: A Doll's House &
       Hedda Gabler

Ibsen's Plays II: Ghosts, An Enemy of
       the People & The Wild Duck

GIANTS IN THE EARTH

NOTES

including
- *Introduction*
- *General Summary*
- *List of Characters*
- *Summaries and Commentaries*
- *Critical Notes*
- *Character Analyses*
- *Questions*
- *Selected Bibliography*

by
Frank B. Huggins

INCORPORATED

LINCOLN, NEBRASKA 68501

Editor

Gary Carey, M.A.
University of Colorado

Consulting Editor

James L. Roberts, Ph.D.
Department of English
University of Nebraska

Cliffs Notes, Inc.   Lincoln, Nebraska

CONTENTS

INTRODUCTION... 5

GENERAL SUMMARY.. 7

CAST OF CHARACTERS... 8

BOOK I

    Chapter I 9

    Chapter II... 12

    Chapter III 15

    Chapter IV...20

    Chapter V 25

    Chapter VI...28

BOOK II

    Chapter I 33

    Chapter II..36

    Chapter III...41

    Chapter IV...45

GENERAL COMMENT.. 49

ANALYSIS OF MAIN CHARACTERS.................................... 50

STYLE.. 52

QUESTIONS AND SUGGESTIONS FOR THEMES................53

GIANTS IN THE EARTH

INTRODUCTION

While this particular novel deals with Norwegian pioneers on the Great Plains in the latter half of the 19th century, it is, in a sense, a story of all the American pioneers that went before them into the west, and is a part of the story of the conquest of the continent.

For every pioneer who succeeded—from Daniel Boone to Sutter in California—there were probably two who fell by the wayside, either physically or emotionally. Per Hansa is the personification of the true pioneer, the strong man who looks into the future and sees a golden life ahead, while Beret, his wife, is torn by doubts, longs for what she has left, and wants only to get away. In a deeper sense it is possibly the story of the caveman and the cavewoman; the male who looked for new adventures and the female who wished only for a comfortable cave in which to rear her young.

The greatness of *Giants in the Earth* is not in the bare bones of the story, for it is a fairly simple one, but in the manner in which Rolvaag manages to bring out the emotions engendered in each of the pioneers—how they reacted to the loneliness and desolation of the prairie and how they adjusted to it or did not adjust, as the case may be.

The conquest of the continent was a great American triumph, but it also took its toll in human lives, misery, and disaster. The wonder of it all is that there were people willing to risk everything they had held dear in order to build a new life. Take one single case in this novel: what on earth impelled the Norwegian with a sick wife and nothing to his name to head west? He had just buried one child in an unknown grave on the prairie and had no idea where he was heading. Per Hansa calls him a "drifter," but in another sense he was a true pioneer.

Where the feeling of the "frontier spirit" originated, no one has satisfactorily explained, but with the crossing of the Allegheny Mountains, following the Revolutionary War, it flowered. Perhaps the early settlers who came from the confined isles of Britain were dazzled with the idea of endless land stretching ahead of them, or possibly it was simply a restlessness that came upon them in this new country. In any case, the breed was born.

There was little to recommend the life, and the American of today would be appalled at the manner in which a pioneer ancestor of his lived. Tragedy was almost a daily occurrence, and hunger a constant companion. Beveridge, in his *Life of Lincoln,* tells us of some of the hardships suffered by the family of our great president. It is not a pleasant story. While this novel is laid a hundred years later, many of the same conditions prevailed. That Beret should go mad in conditions that she had only known in nightmares is understandable, and was probably true of hundreds of other pioneer women who put up with the wilderness while their husbands literally carved out their dreams. To the strong man, physical action was the panacea, but this did not apply to the women who longed for something more. Some became hard and calloused, but most of them accepted their lot and toiled and suffered and died so that they might bring up their children in the promised land their men envisaged.

While the stories are not similar, it is interesting to note that Knut Hamsun, the great Norwegian writer and Nobel Prize winner, wrote several stories about Norwegian pioneers in his own country. The classic is *Growth of the Soil,* in which a couple carve out a homestead in virgin territory. The protagonists were hardy people, similar to the Norwegian immigrants who conquered the Great Plains in this country, and a parallel might be drawn.

The Norwegians who settled in the Great Plains were a small but vital part of the immigrants who poured through Ellis Island in the 19th century and enriched America. Rolvaag knows of what he writes, and he writes with affection and understanding.

Ole Edvart Rolvaag was himself a viking of the Per Hansa strain. Born of fisherfolk in 1876 on the island of Donna at the very edge of the Arctic Circle, he was, from the age of fourteen, a fisherman around the Lofoten Islands — one of the roughest of all professions. In 1896 he came to the United States, tried his hand at farming in South Dakota, then decided to get an education at St. Olaf College in Minnesota. After further education at the University of Oslo in Norway, he returned to his American alma mater and eventually became professor of Norwegian Literature.

It is interesting to note that this novel about Americans in America was originally written in Norwegian, first published in Norway, and later translated into English.

GENERAL SUMMARY

This is the story of the early Norwegian settlers on the Great Plains and of the travail they went through in trying to build a settlement and farm the virgin land.

Per Hansa, the male protagonist, is the natural pioneer who looks to the future and believes that he can accomplish anything if only he works hard enough. His wife, Beret, on the other hand, longs for the homeland she left to follow her husband.

The action takes place in the 1870's and the locale is South Dakota.

Per Hansa, his friend Hans Olsa who has been a fisherman like him back in Norway, Tonseten, and the Solum boys, as they are called, start the work of conquering the prairie.

In time they all prosper to an extent and Per Hansa is particularly pleased with the way things are going except for his growing concern over his wife's strange ways. Finally, when a plague of grasshoppers descends on them and ravages the fields, Beret loses her mind and only regains her sanity later after an itinerant minister visits the settlement and helps her spiritually. This, and the knowledge that her husband loves her deeply, brings her back to a more-or-less normal state.

Then comes the terrible winter of 1880-81 when almost every day from October to April there is a blizzard. One day Hans Olsa is caught out in it and taken very ill. Both he and Beret want Per Hansa to go for a minister, but Per Hansa feels it is impossible to travel in this weather. In the end, however, he sets out on skis—and is found dead later in the spring.

CAST OF CHARACTERS

Per Hansa
The male protagonist, strong and virile, the natural pioneer.

Beret
Per Hansa's wife, who hungers for home and hates the Great Plains.

Ole (or Olamand)
Oldest son of the family.

Anna Marie (And-Ongen, the "Duckling")
The daughter.

Hans Kristian (Store-Hans, meaning "Big Hans")
The second son.

Hans Olsa
Friend of Per Hansa and nominal leader of the group.

Sorrina
Hans Olsa's wife.

Syvert Tonseten
One of the settlers, a weak man.

Kjersti Tonseten
His wife, a kindly and wise woman.

The Solums (Henry and Sam)
Two bachelor brothers who are in the settlement. They are the only ones that are proficient in English.

Peder Victorius
Beret and Per Hansa's youngest son.

Tronders and Helgelaendings
Names of Norwegian clans.

The Minister
Not identified by name, an itinerant minister who moves from settlement to settlement.

BOOK I

CHAPTER I

TOWARD THE SUNSET

Summary
A caravan, consisting of two dilapidated wagons drawn by oxen and followed by a tethered cow, makes its way through the tall grass of the Great Plains. Walking ahead of it is Per Hansa, a Norwegian immigrant, who with his family and all his earthly possessions, was moving west from Minnesota to Dakota Territory. His family consists of his wife Beret, his two sons Ole and Hans, and his daughter Anna Marie.

For more than three weeks the caravan had been painfully crawling across the plain. As of the moment Per Hansa knows he is lost, for he had gotten off the trail and could only hope that by heading west he would reach Split Rock Creek soon. Ahead of them are other Norwegian pioneers from whom they have become separated. Beret wonders if they will ever see the others again, and Per Hansa tries to console her by saying that as long as they head towards the sunset they will eventually meet. Towards sunset, Hans, who has been walking ahead with his father, says he sees a wood ahead and wonders if there are people there. Per Hansa decides to stop for the night.

They prepare their campsite and each of them performs his chores. The fire is made and Beret waits for the pot to boil. Hans wanders off up a hill, but when he sees how far he has come from the wagons, he is afraid and returns quickly. They eat supper, which consists of porridge and milk. After supper they watch the moon rise over the plains and Per Hansa orders the children to go to sleep. Per Hansa smokes his pipe and after the children have gone to sleep Beret asks him if he thinks they will ever find the others again. Per Hansa says he is sure of it.

Although Per Hansa pretends to sleep, he lies awake for a long time, staring into the night. He is gnawed by doubts, about whether he should ever have started on this journey, and he recalls how his wife had had grave misgivings about the venture. He remembers with dismay how his wagon had been wrecked, and he had had to put back to Jackson for repairs while the others went on ahead. His friend, Hans Olsa, had wanted to wait for him, but Per Hansa had insisted he go on ahead. And now he was lost. Per Hansa wonders why he had ever left Fillmore County. He should have stayed until his wife had had her child and then moved west in the spring.

When he feels sure that everyone is sleeping, Per Hansa dresses and goes off to examine the ground they will travel the next day. He goes over a ridge and finds an abandoned campsite and some fresh horse dung. He goes on to find a ford across the creek; he finds it, wades across, and finds a dried mutton leg that he knows belonged to Hans Olsa. Per Hansa is happy now, for he knows he has found the trail. He returns to the camp to find Beret awake. She has been terrified to find him gone, and Per Hansa comforts her.

Commentary

In these early short chapters Rolvaag sets the scene of the Great Plains in the days before they were settled. The picture we get is one of desolation, of a sea of grass through which a solitary family caravan moves slowly. At the same time the author is building up the character of his protagonists. In the beginning the protagonist is clearly Per Hansa, the Norwegian pioneer, eager to take up land and build himself a home.

Time and again we are reminded of how miserably frail and weak this small caravan is against the forces of nature personified by the great, vast country. But at the same time, while we are shown that Per Hansa has his doubts, his strength of character is being brought out. He is at heart an optimist and sure that he will eventually reach the others of the group who have gone ahead of him because of the accident he had had with his wagon.

In contrast, while it is not brought out strongly yet, we see that Per Hansa's wife, Beret, has doubts that are much deeper, that she already feels a hatred for this desolate land. It is only because her man had wanted to push westward that Beret had come; she has no desire to make a home in this country. At the end of the first book we see Beret's fears come to the surface when she thinks that Per Hansa has left her.

The opening chapters are in essence a masterful description of the Great Plains and an introduction to the character of the two protagonists, Beret and Per Hansa. At this point, more has been said about Per Hansa, but the book is actually a saga of Beret as will become evident.

While the plot lines are in no way similar, the opening of Rolvaag's book is reminiscent of Knut Hamsun's (Nobel Prize for Literature, 1920) *Growth of the Soil,* in which the great Norwegian author tells the tale of Norwegian pioneers heading north in their own country.

At this point the supernatural is not brought out yet, but Beret's misgivings as they head into the unknown are laying the foundation for what will come later.

12

CHAPTER II

HOME-FOUNDING

Summary

On the side of a hill near a creek that winds its way through the prairie, Hans Olsa is building a sod house. He stops now and then to search for something. Beyond the half-completed sod house a tent has been pitched, and around it are some rough pieces of furniture. In the neighborhood other sod huts are rising. Hans Olsa's wife calls him to dinner in the tent and asks if he has seen anything. He answers in the negative, and after eating he returns to his work. His wife tells him that he should go looking for Per Hansa, but Hans Olsa says he has no idea where to search. As they are talking, Syvert Tonseten turns up and asks if they have seen anything of "them." When Hans Olsa asks in turn if Tonseten has seen them, the latter says that he has had them in sight for over an hour. Hans Olsa and his wife face in the direction Tonseten indicates, and they see a small caravan coming across the plains. Within a half hour Per Hansa and his family arrive to be welcomed with open arms by the earlier arrivals. There is general rejoicing, but in the midst of it Beret has a feeling that there is something wrong with the place. She feels the immensity of the plains and is appalled by it. Hans Olsa tells Per Hansen that he has laid out stakes for a quarter section next to him.

The small group of pioneers sit around and celebrate the arrival of Per Hansa and his family until Per Hansa concludes the celebration by saying that he wants to see his quarter. Hans Olsa tells Per Hansa he must go into Sioux Falls the next day and file his claim to the land. Per Hansa, Hans Olsa, and Tonseten go together and look over the land. Per Hansa discovers an old Indian grave and is vaguely troubled by it, but he is elated that this land is to be his.

The next morning Per Hansa and one of the Solum boys go into Sioux Falls and file his claim. The date on it is June 6, 1873. In the meantime, Beret and the boys unload the wagons and set the larger one up as a bedroom. All the while she is working she feels a certain unease that she cannot pinpoint. After the work is done and supper is finished, Beret climbs to the highest point on their land and surveys the plains. She admits that it has a certain beauty, but she finds the silence, the great open spaces, depressing. Again she thinks that there is nothing to hide behind. The full extent of her loneliness hits her. She recalls how they had left Norway and come to Quebec, then pushed ever westward. Finally they came to Fillmore County in Minnesota, but even that was not to be their stopping place. Now she was here in the middle of an endless prairie. When she returns to the wagon, the boys bring her some stones they have found and Beret examines them. She asks the boys where they had found the stones and follows them to the place—the grave Per Hansa had found the day before. That night Beret is unable to sleep for a long time.

Per Hansa returns the next day from Sioux Falls in a buoyant and conquering mood. He is wrapped up in his future plans, and Beret feels she cannot get through to him. Per Hansa tells her that he has bought ten sacks of potatoes and is going to plant them before he starts to build a house. Per Hansa lies in bed that night and thinks of all the things he needs and the things that he must do. And he thinks of the baby that Beret is going to have shortly and of the house that he will build her someday.

In the morning Per Hansa goes over to Hans Olsa's to borrow his plow. He hitches up the oxen and starts the first furrow on his new land. By breakfast time he has made a fine start, and after breakfast he takes the two boys with him to break up the sod and lead the oxen. At noon they return with sod for the future house, and Per Hansa puts in a full afternoon's work. He feels that he must use every minute of time available.

That same evening Per Hansa begins to build the sod hut although Beret begs him to rest. After this, Per Hansa works on the house every morning before breakfast and every evening after supper, and he is busy every minute of the day. Beret wants him to rest, but there is a drive in him that he cannot curb, and before long he has laid down his field and built his sod hut. Beret is tired out with the labor she had undergone, but she is happy for Per Hansa.

When Per Hansa's sod house is complete except for the roof, Tonseten tells him that it is much too large to thatch. Tonseten thinks that Per Hansa has done a crazy thing in building such a big house. But Per Hansa had thought for a long time about the problem of building a sod house, and he had decided that it should be large enough to be house and barn under one roof. Beret is at first troubled by the idea of man and beast in one building, but then she thinks of how desolate and lonesome everything was here and she thinks of how comfortable a companion Rosie the cow might be on a cold winter evening.

One evening some time later Per Hansa goes to Hans Olsa's to borrow his new wagon. Per Hansa plans to go to the Sioux River some 25 miles away to see if there are big stands of timber that he has heard about. Per Hansa decides to take the younger son, Hans, with him, and this is a blow to Ole, the older. Beret is not happy about the trip; also she knows they must have wood for a roof for the sod house. By the third day after Per Hansa and Hans have left, Beret is almost in a panic and she goes to see Hans Olsa, but Per Hansa arrives the next day with a load so big that the oxen were barely able to drag it. Included in the timber load that would serve as a roof and winter fuel, were six bundles of young trees to be planted around the house, and in addition a dozen young plum trees. Per Hansa had made the acquaintance of another group of Norwegian settlers on the Sioux River, and in time this was to have great significance.

Commentary

From the near-tragedy of the opening chapter we now come to the rhapsody of the meeting of the pioneers in their new lands. The men are happy; they are reunited, and ahead of them lies only work so that they may make a home of this wilderness. Through it all, however, Beret is assailed with doubts. The phrase: "Why, there isn't even a thing that one can hide behind," should be kept in mind. This is the obsession that is to haunt Beret.

The attitude of the pioneer man and his woman who follows him is now being brought out more clearly. Per Hansa is happy and eager to get to work to clear his land, to build a home and to get ready for whatever may come. Beret, on the other hand, is more and more assailed by doubts. She longs for the life she had had in Norway and dreads this vast, desolate land.

The incident of the old Indian grave is not in itself significant, but it should be borne in mind that the Norwegians (Scandinavians in general) had a deep superstitious nature going back to the ancient Sagas, and anything that they considered an ill omen weighed on their minds. Per Hansa, while he dismisses what the others consider an omen of sorts, is vaguely troubled by the presence of the Indian grave, while Beret is deeply troubled. To her it is definitely a bad omen.

These are the passages in which the vigor of Per Hansa is most displayed. Nothing is too much for him: he plows and he builds and he plans, and everything he does comes out right. Beret is still doubtful, but at this point she plays a very secondary role to her masterful husband.

CHAPTER III

ROSIE! – ROSIE!

Summary
As the summer wore on, the settlers' food supplies steadily vanished. The time had come to take a trip into town, but this was no simple undertaking. While no one wished to acknowledge it they all realized that they were living in a land where man's strength availed but little. On top of this there was fear of the Indians; the men never spoke of them while the women were around, but they were aware that their colony was in the path of an Indian trail that led to Nebraska. It is decided that Hans Olsa and Tonseten and Henry Solum, each of whom owned horses and wagons, would make up the party for the journey into town. Per Hansa is out of sorts, for he feels he should have been included. He takes out his ill humor in work and plows an acre and a half of prairie, a record that stood for many years.

The next day Per Hansa puts in another good day's work, and as he and Ole return home, Hans comes running to meet them and announces that people are coming. Beret resignedly says "they have come," but Per Hansa tells her to prepare supper as if nothing had happened. Per Hansa prepares his rifle and watches the approaching train, but shortly his anxiety wanes and he decides that it is nothing but harmless Indian families moving across the Great Plains. Once Per Hansa has made up his mind, he is calm, but this is not true of his neighbors, Sam Solum and Tonseten's wife, Kjersti. Per Hansa works on his sod house, but he sends Hans to collect the women.

The Indian band approaches, goes over the summit of the hill and stops. The Indians release their horses to graze, and this act reassures Per Hansa. At this moment Sorine's cow galloped away toward the wagons of the newcomers. This starts a stampede of all the cows in the colony. Beret says that one of the men must go after the cows, and Per Hansa says he will do so after they have eaten. Per Hansa jokes about how Indians like to take the scalps of cows, but Beret is not amused and berates him. Per Hansa is deeply hurt, and goes off with Hans to see the Indians.

Hans is excited at the prospect of meeting the Indians, but Per Hansa can only think of how Beret had spoken harshly to him in front of the others. They come to the Indian encampment and find several wigwams, squaws busy around a fire and Indians sitting around smoking pipes. Per Hansa is unable to communicate with them because he knows little English, but Hans manages to convey that they live here. Per Hansa realizes all he has to do is to round up the four stray cows and drive them home, but he is reluctant to do so; he has not had a smoke of tobacco in a long time, and the odor from the Indian's pipes holds him captive. Finally, he pulls out his pipe and indicates to one of the Indians that he would like to fill it. The Indian hands him a pouch of tobacco and Per Hansa fills his pipe. He lights it and feels a rare contentment.

As he is enjoying his smoke Per Hansa notices an Indian lying by the fire who is in obvious agony. He tells Hans to ask what is the matter with the man and learns that his hand is hurt; Per Hansa says he wants to take a look at it. Per Hansa examines the Indian's hand and decides that it is a case of blood poisoning, or close to it. Per Hansa sends Hans back to bring white cloths, and if possible some liquor from Hans Olsa's. He works on the hand, drawing on the experience he gathered as a fisherman in Norway. Hans returns, bringing Beret with him; she tells Per Hansa he must return at once, that the women of the colony are very disturbed. But Per Hansa pays no attention to her and continues to minister to the Indian; he gets Beret to help him. After he has worked on the wound for a while he tells Beret to go home and take Hans with her; he will return later with the cows.

Per Hansa continues to look after the sick Indian, changing the dressing from time to time. The other Indians are all asleep, when Beret returns. She has been crying, but she stays on as Per Hansa continues his doctoring. The Indians bring Per Hansa and Beret blankets, and they sleep around the fire. The Indians remained for another day and night, and the sick Indian's hand, while not fully healed, seemed much better. Before they left, the sick Indian comes to Per Hansa's home leading a fully saddled pony and presents it to him. The boys, Hans and Ole, are delighted, and Per Hansa is flabbergasted.

On the following day the wagons arrived from town bringing all matter of merchandise, including a plow and a rake for Per Hansa. The storekeeper in town had sold this on credit to Hans Olsa, and Per Hansa is interested to know whether the man will extend further credit, for he needs other things and has run out of the small amount of cash he had. The returned voyagers, however, are more interested in what had happened while they had been gone. Per Hansa insists that his dealings with the Indians were nothing. The men celebrate the return of the expedition by drinking together in Hans Olsa's barn. Hans Olsa's wife, Sorine, finds two bottles in one of the boxes her husband had brought back, and she pours a drink for both of the neighboring women. There is a general celebration.

The work in the settlement continues, and everyone is busy at his various chores when suddenly one noon Tonseten's wife, Kjersti, notices that her cow is missing. She sounds the alarm and they all realize that the cows have gone. The search is on, but the cows are not found.

That evening, outside of every hut the settlers stood watching, but no cows appeared. Everyone feels a deep sense of gloom. The families gather and decide that the cows must have been taken by the Indians. They tell Per Hansa that it is his responsibility to find the Indians and get the cows back, but this angers Per Hansa and he leaves the group.

Rest was a long time in coming to them at Per Hansa's that night. Hans is heartbroken at the loss of his beloved cow, Rosie, and Per Hansa comforts him as best he can. Hans asks if Indians scalp cows and Per Hansa tells him no, that Indians are nice people. With this reassurance, Hans falls asleep.

At the first light of dawn Per Hansa is awake and readying himself to go and hunt for the cows. Beret is already awake; she has not slept, plagued by the surroundings in which she lives, the dread she has for this endless, empty country. This is no place for human beings to dwell, she tells herself, and then, what of the children? In a sense she feels that the loss of cows might be a blessing and that her husband would come to his senses and leave this desolate land. Beret asks Per Hansa what he intends to do and when he tells her that he is going to ride eastward to search for the cows she tells him he is doing a wrong thing. She berates him for leaving her alone, saying that one of the others could go. Per Hansa cannot understand what is the matter with Beret; it bothers him deeply.

Before Per Hansa can get on his pony, Hans Olsa appears and asks him if he is going after the cows. Per Hansa answers in the affirmative, and Hans Olsa says that his wife had remarked the night before that perhaps the cows were wanting male company. They laugh at the thought, but Per Hansa says he will visit the Tronders (the Norwegian settlement on the Sioux River). He asks Hans Olsa to keep an eye on things. As he rides off onto the prairie, Beret looks after him, crying. Tonseten is angry at Per Hansa because he thinks that the latter has not the courage to go after the Indians. Everyone in the small settlement is sad at the loss of the cattle, and while they all gather at Beret's they find her manner unnatural and disturbing. After everyone has left, Beret prepares for sleep. She tries to shut out the prairie by hanging clothes at the window and barring the door.

The following day Per Hansa's boys climb up on the roof to look for him. Sometime in the afternoon, Hans sights his father and screams out the news. He says that the cattle are with him, and the two boys slide down from the roof to spread the news. The settlement watches as Per Hansa drives the cows before him, but they are surprised to see that instead of four there are now five cows. But before the arrival of Per Hansa they realize that the fifth beast is not a cow but a yearling bull. Per Hansa is weary to the point of stupor. He has with him a cage of sorts in which there are two hens and a rooster. Per Hansa explains to the others that he talked a Tronder woman into letting him have the bull for a year for ten dollars, and that this would be cheaper than chasing their cows all over the Dakota Territory.

Commentary

These are not particularly significant chapters in advancing the story of the pioneers, but they bring to the fore again the strength of Per Hansa and his ability to cope with the Great Plains. The Indian interlude is actually just that; while the others might have felt dread for the Indians. Per Hansa is unafraid and secure in the knowledge that they speak the same language in their hearts.

The whole episode of Per Hansa and the sick Indian and of the cows is nothing but a device by which Rolvaag is building up the character of a brave and resourceful man. But at the same time, the author is stressing the dread that Beret has for the Great Plains country, for the desolate land that she is unused to.

In an indirect way we are given a glimpse of Per Hansa's past; when ministering to the sick Indian, we gather that Per Hansa has been at one time a fisherman on the Lofoten seas, and that Hans Olsa has been his companion. Lofoten is a herring fishing area in the north of Norway, and a particularly rugged one where only the hardiest of fishermen venture.

Again, these chapters are building up the strong character of Per Hansa, the pioneer who looks upon the new land as a challenge and one that he welcomes. His boys go along with him, but the woman—personified in Beret—does not. She is troubled at every new thing that happens, longs for a home that is thousands of miles across the sea, and cannot understand why her beloved husband is happy in this sea of grass.

CHAPTER IV

WHAT THE WAVING GRASS REVEALED

Summary

Per Hansa is wrapped up in the work of building his estate and is happier than he has ever been. He works endlessly and only rests when fatigue overcomes him. As he works on his quarter section he envisions a day when he will have another quarter section on which he will keep cattle and other livestock. Per Hansa dreams, too, of the house that he will build for Beret; he is restless, always working, always planning.

One Sunday evening the boys return to the house and tell of a swamp they found where there were thousands of ducks. Per Hansa says that he cannot use what little ammunition he has for his shotgun, so the ducks will have to wait. But one Sunday, Per Hansa goes with Hans to see them, and he tries to figure some way in which they could be caught. On the way home from the trip, Per Hansa makes a startling discovery. He decides to pace down the western border of his and Tonseten's land. At Tonseten's southwest corner Per Hansa's foot comes up against a stake in the grass; Per Hansa is rather surprised to think that his friend Tonseten would be so careful of his boundaries and takes a good look at the stake. He is shocked to find that the stake has a name on it that is not Tonseten's but simply O'Hara. After the initial shock, Per Hansa paces along the boundary line between Tonseten's and Hans Olsa's quarter and finds another stake with the name Joe Gill on it. He makes a further search but cannot find a stake by his land. The Per Hansa who had been so lighthearted a few hours earlier, comes home with a weariness greater than he had ever known.

To Per Hansa the discovery of the stakes is so disheartening that he can only think that the trolls have come to his beloved land. The next morning Per Hansa is up very early and leaves the house. Beret watches him go striding off to the west and wonders what he is up to; she feels that something is wrong. Later, he returns, eats breakfast and goes off again, this time with the boys. Going to his own south line, he tells the boys to hunt for a black stake in the grass. They comb the whole area, and when they find nothing, Per Hansa is almost joyful.

Beret soon comes to realize that Per Hansa is keeping something from her, and she wonders what on earth there is to conceal out on the prairie. For a week Beret feels no communication between them. On the next Monday, Per Hansa gets up before daylight, takes a spade and goes off to the stakes he found on the boundaries of his friends. He pulls them out, works the ground so that there will be no evidence of a stake ever having been there, and is very careful not to trample down the grass. Later, Per Hansa takes the boys out to do some plowing, and Beret happens to go to the stable and discovers the stakes. They puzzle her, but she does not realize what they are until later she sees Per Hansa chopping them up and burning them. Then it comes to her that Per Hansa is meddling with other folks' landmarks, one of the blackest of sins. Beret can hardly sleep that night, but Per Hansa sleeps well.

Per Hansa is driven by a furious energy to get as much done in as short a time as possible. Before him is the thought at all times of what he will do when the trolls come. At first he wonders if perhaps the stakes had been put in before Tonseten arrived and no claim had been filed, but he soon dismisses this thought and realizes that the stakes had not been in the ground that long. There was nothing to do but wait for them to come back. He says nothing to anyone. In the meantime, Beret is trying to reconcile herself to what she knows her husband has done. She reasons that perhaps on these wide prairies, there is more than enough land for everyone, but she is still not satisfied, and Per Hansa continues to be difficult to live with.

Beret forms the habit of looking at the prairie, at the whole compass, and her depression grows; they have been there four months and in that time the only strangers they have seen have been the Indians. She begins to brood more than ever, but quite unexpectedly one day a covered wagon appears on the prairie and ends up at Tonseten's. All the members of the small community rush there to see what sort of people have come. The newcomers turn out to be four German men who are going on further west to find land on which to settle. They stay the night, and in the morning Per Hansa shows them his house and stable under one roof, and he sells them two dollars and seventy-five cents worth of potatoes, which is the first produce to be sold out of the settlement on Spring Creek.

The strangers leave the next day, but their visit has affected everyone in the settlement in different ways. To Per Hansa it means that now there are settlers on all sides of them; he feels confident that he will live to see the day when most of the land of the prairie will be taken up. But to Beret the visit is nothing but a brief interruption to the endless solitude. About a week later, another caravan arrived, consisting this time of six wagons; they do not come to the settlement but set up a camp some distance off. Per Hansa and Tonseten pay them a visit, and while Per Hansa cannot speak English he soon gathers that Tonseten is very angry. Tonseten tells Per Hansa that these people claim all the land between the creek and the swamp over to the westward. The newcomers are Irish and a wild bunch, and when the Norwegians start to leave, one of them trips Per Hansa, and he turns on the fellow and threatens to hit him. No one wants anything to do with the huge Per Hansa, and he and Tonseten go their way after deciding that the menfolk will meet in the morning to discuss what is to be done.

Per Hansa returns from the camp, quite happy with the turn of events. He is convinced that the Irish newcomers have no legitimate claim to the land. Beret notices the change in mood in Per Hansa and realizes that no danger hangs over them. Beret and the boys want to know about the people in the camp, and Per Hansa tells them that they are Irish and are not going to settle here. The next morning, before anyone else is awake, Per Hansa goes to the Solum boys' place and awakens them. As the three of them walk to Hans Olsa's, Per Hansa tells the Solums about the situation, explaining that while the three of them have nothing to worry about, their neighbors are in trouble. He asks the Solums to act as interpreters in their dealing with the Irish. Per Hansa tells them that they must check the papers of the Irish to see that they have not been tampered with; he adds that he intends to stay where he is until he is kicked out bodily.

When Per Hansa reaches Hans Olsa's house, he finds that both Hans Olsa and his wife, Sorine, are awake. Per Hansa does not wish to speak of the matter before Sorine, but soon realizes that he must explain the trouble quickly. Hans Olsa, a giant of a man with a slow-thinking mind, wishes to think over things, but Per Hansa tells him to get his deed and hurry over to the newcomer's camp. After Hans Olsa finally realizes that the Irish want to kick him off his land, he agrees to go.

Tonseten and the Solum boys are impatient to get the business over at once, but Per Hansa insists that they must have a plan. Per Hansa explains the tactics they must use: Henry Solum and Tonseten should be the spokesmen, Sam Solum the interpreter. When they arrive at the camp they find that the strangers are already fully awake. Per Hansa tells his companions that the first thing they must demand is to see the papers and then the stakes—particularly the stakes. The strangers do not take kindly to this, and finally say that the papers had been packed away somewhere and could not be immediately found. But, says one, he will show them the stakes. He starts off, and the Norwegians follow him. But when the stranger comes to the place at Hans Olsa's southwest corner, he can find nothing. Eventually, the Irish give up and go back to their camp, followed by Per Hansa and his companions. When they reach the camp the strangers—ten of them—are in an ugly mood and accuse the Norwegians of destroying another man's landmarks. One of the strangers comes at Hans Olsa with a sledgehammer, but the giant takes him bodily and throws him at one of the wagons. The fight is over. That afternoon, Per Hansa returns to the camp to find that the strangers have moved further west. He sells them ten dollars worth of potatoes, and feels that he has struck up a profitable business. The Irish settle on the two quarters west of the settlement, but leave before the snow. The following spring they come back with a large company and start their permanent settlement.

On the morning when the men go out to parley with the Irish, Kjersti—Tonseten's wife—is left all alone in the house. The night before, Tonseten had told her of what had happened, and his misery was such that they had had little sleep. After her husband leaves, Kjersti goes over to see Beret, but she gets little comfort there and discovers that Per Hansa has not told her of the trouble. When Beret hears the story from Kjersti, she is again struck by a sense of horror that Per Hansa destroyed the stakes and is now planning to drive the people from their land. Kjersti returns home to find Tonseten moaning and groaning about how terrible things are. Tonseten tells Kjersti about the fight and says that from now on everything will be a mess and they might as well move back to the east. Later, he is told that the Irish have moved on. For a long time the Irish were the standing topic of discussion in the little settlement. But the only one who does not talk about them is Beret, who is obsessed by the thought that her husband had destroyed the stakes and kept it a secret from everyone, including her. She feels that she cannot endure life in such a place. One afternoon the Irish come over to Per Hansa's to buy some potatoes, and that evening the settlement comes over to find out how they had behaved. Per Hansa says they are fine people, and he then tells the story of the stakes. Hans Olsa and Tonseten praise him for his action, but Beret berates them for condoning what she still considers a heinous crime. During the days that followed, words were few and distant between Per Hansa and Beret.

Commentary

The chapter starts on a high and joyous note, and is focused on Per Hansa and his work. The author shows us a happy and busy man, building for the present, planning for the future. The discovery of the ducks in the swamp is another pleasant thing. Then abruptly the mood changes when Per Hansa discovers the boundary stakes on his friends' land.

Here we have not only the sudden change in mood, but the delineation of character between Per Hansa and Beret that will become more and more evident as the story moves along. Per Hansa is the man of action; he is willing to face facts and to do something. Beret is the brooder, the thinker, the mystic. The destruction of the stakes is a good case in point: presumably Per Hansa is aware of the enormity of his crime by old country standards, but he is willing to take a chance for the sake of his friends. Beret, on the other hand can only think of what Per Hansa has done, and does not take into consideration what might have motivated the act. When the matter of the land is settled and the disgruntled Irish would-be claim jumpers move on, everyone—with one exception—praises Per Hansa for what he did. Beret is the only one who cannot condone what was quite apparently a very wise move; to her the crime is no less because the result turned out favorably.

Here, the story begins to examine Beret more fully. Up to this point it has been all Per Hansa; now, Rolvaag begins to probe more deeply into his protagonists' souls. It is no longer simply an action story.

Here, too, the trolls enter the story. Trolls, in Scandinavian folklore are dwarfish or gigantic inhabitants of caves in the mountains. Generally, they are evil creatures, although on occasion they are friendly to human beings. They are found all through Norwegian literature. In Ibsen's *Peer Gynt,* for example, the mountain king is a troll. In Sigrid Undset's Nobel Prize winning work, the monumental *Kristin Lavransdatter,* the heroine is often bothered by the thought of evil trolls working on her. The Scandinavians have been Christians for centuries, but apparently the memory of the earlier myths is hard to erase.

Finally, as the chapter ends, we see that Beret and Per Hansa are beginning to drift apart. Beret increasingly feels the dread of the empty prairie, while to Per Hansa it remains a magnificent challenge, to be met and conquered through work. While generalizations might be dangerous, Rolvaag is quite possibly simply pointing out the difference between a man and a woman.

CHAPTER V

FACING THE GREAT DESOLATION

Summary
In the beginning of October, one day Per Hansa, Hans Olsa, and Henry Solum go east to the Sioux River after wood. Beret sits at home knitting, her mood of melancholy deeper than ever. She looks out over the prairie and sees a wagon train approaching. Beret feels that she should do something to turn the people back, to tell

them to stay away from the wilderness. But Hans is excited and rides off to tell Tonseten.

When the strangers arrive, it is discovered that they are all Norwegians. Tonseten is delighted, although he wishes that Per Hansa were there to do the honors. He insists that the newcomers sleep in his house before moving west to look for homesteads. The next day the would-be settlers go out to look at the land and Tonseten does everything in his power to persuade them to settle in the area. After looking over the available sites the majority of the newcomers decide it would be a good place to settle. They intend to return in the spring with their families. Tonseten is delighted at the thought of a growing Norwegian community.

The time comes when Per Hansa finds it necessary to go into town to get needed provisions. This time he will be gone a week, and Beret dreads the thought of being on the prairie without him. Thanks to the potatoes that he had sold the Irish and the newly-arrived Norwegians, Per Hansa's cash supply is a good deal larger than when he had first arrived in early summer. Before his father leaves, Hans tells him he is worried about Beret, and Per Hansa tells the boy that there may be a little one coming along around Christmas time. Per Hansa finds he has more potatoes than he needs, and loads his wagon with the surplus to try and sell in town.

Per Hansa and his companions are happy to be going to town. At the Sioux River they catch three fish, and that night when they stop at Split Rock Creek they eat the fish with potatoes. The next morning they continue their journey and discover that in the wilderness they had seen in the summer there are now numerous sod huts of settlers. Late in the forenoon they come across two sod huts and find that they are inhabited by a Norwegian couple who have nothing but a pair of oxen and a cow. Per Hansa senses that they are short of food and gives them a generous supply of his potatoes. He is happy that he has been able to do something for others.

When they reach Worthington, a frontier settlement on the railroad line, Per Hansa tries to peddle his potatoes but has little luck until he meets a Danish widow who trades him three chickens for some of his potatoes. The widow asks Per Hansa to stay for dinner, and he consents; he is impressed by the interior of her sod hut, which is white, and discovers that it is whitewashed. After the meal, Per Hansa goes to a lumberman the widow had told him about and barters potatoes for lime and lumber. Later, Per Hansa trades for a plow and rake on credit and for net twine and rope. Finally, Per Hansa asks for some calico of a gaudy pattern, ribbon and thread, then cloth, and tobacco, and matches, and kerosene, and molasses, and salt. After the everyday needs were looked after, the men buy several bottles of liquor. Late in the afternoon they set off for home. They are all happy, and when they pitch camp for the first night, Per Hansa starts to knit the twine into a net.

The boys find the days long while their father is gone, and Beret says little to them to brighten their days. Then they hear that Tonseten has killed a bear; they go to his place and receive a pail of "bear" meat, bring it home and give it to Beret. They ask her if they can take the old shotgun and go after the mother bear, but Beret flies into a rage and beats them with a switch—something that has never happened before in their lives. Beret makes a stew of the meat, with potatoes and carrots, but when it comes time to eat the boys say that it cannot be bear, but badger, and no one can eat the meal. Beret throws it out, and later she hangs more clothes over the window and sits up very late, unable to sleep.

That night Beret is unable to sleep. The thought of the badger that they had almost eaten is the last straw as far as she is concerned. They must go back east, leave this desolate place. In the morning Beret worries about the lack of wagons, but feels that that is Per Hansa's problem. She begins to pack the few belongings they have and Hans realizes that something is wrong. He tries to comfort his mother, and succeeds in doing so to an extent. Beret cries, and feels the baby moving within her. At that moment Ole comes running in to say that the caravan is returning.

At dinner after Per Hansa returns, he is very happy and tells the boys of his adventure. Even Beret smiles at the way in which the boys receive the tale. In turn, the boys tell their father about Tonseten and the badger and he laughs in turn. After dinner Per Hansa and the boys bring in things from the wagon, and Per Hansa insists that Beret have a drink. Per Hansa is so happy and irresistible that Beret for a time feels as she had in the past. The boys are put to work knitting the net, and Per Hansa busies himself making ready to mix the lime he had bought in town. After the boys are asleep, Per Hansa continues to work on the net and tells Beret how he intends to catch fish with it. The fact of the matter is he intends to catch ducks with it, but he wishes to keep this his secret. That night, Beret sleeps well, without covering the window.

Commentary

Here again, Rolvaag works on the picture he has been painting all along—of Per Hansa, the man of action who is in his element in the wilderness and happy so long as he has something to do, and of Beret who is growing more and more obsessed by the desolate country. While the author does not belabor the point we are struck by the fact that while Per Hansa, with each passing day, is adjusting to the environment, exactly the opposite is true of Beret.

In the beginning of the chapter we are told of how new settlers are coming all the time; to Per Hansa this is a good thing, but to Beret it only means that others are coming to suffer along with her.

This is the main theme. Note how Per Hansa is constantly thinking of what he can do to make life better for his family in a material way. He purchases various things in town and plans to whitewash the sod hut so that it will be more liveable. Note that all this pertains to the material—or pragmatical—side of things, while Beret is concerned with the emotional, the spiritual. While the chapter ends on a more-or-less happy emotional note, it is clear that Beret is increasingly unhappy about the wilderness life, and her pregnancy adds nothing to make her cheerful. On the other hand Per Hansa is climbing and obviously feels that he is on the way to building his dream empire.

CHAPTER VI

THE HEART THAT DARED NOT LET IN THE SUN

Summary

Autumn comes to the plains, and brings with it a further feeling of desolation. The skies darken, and everything is gray. The snow falls, and in the morning there is light, but no sun. The wind howls and the snow falls.

Per Hansa and the boys work hard preparing for winter, and they are happy, but Beret cannot share their mood. She admits, however, that Per Hansa has achieved wonders, the whitewashed walls being one thing. She is thankful, too, for the fish that Per Hansa and the boys caught with the net that they fashioned. But the crowning glory of the net so far as the males are concerned is the way in which they are catching ducks. Beret cannot share their triumph and complains that they cannot possibly eat so many fowl. Winter arrives, and everyone in the settlement is busy with his own tasks. There is little visiting back and forth, and even less at Per Hansa's, for they all wonder what is wrong with Beret. But after the boys deliver gifts of ducks to the others, they all come over to find out how Per Hansa had caught them. They are all amazed at the whitewash on his walls, and praise it highly. Hans Olsa is somewhat bothered that his best friend, Per Hansa, has kept it a secret from him.

Winter comes, and Per Hansa finds he cannot get enough work. He sleeps after every meal and is fretful that there is nothing to do outside. Finally, Per Hansa takes the boys with him and they work on the woodpile, but after four days this palls, and the feeling of desolation is on them again. Then Tonseten and his wife Kjersti come to visit and they all talk of the old days in Norway. Later, Hans Olsa's household drop by, and they are concerned about Beret and her state of health. Per Hansa is overjoyed that people have come by, and he brings out the frozen fish so that they can all have a feast.

By November the winter has been with them for what seems a long time. Per Hansa worries about Beret, who is like a stranger to him now. Per Hansa notices that whenever he shows Beret any tenderness, she bursts into tears, and he is deeply worried. Per Hansa is further troubled that Beret, who had always been neat, now does not care about how she looks; he brings it to her attention, and Beret spends a long time tidying herself, but the change is temporary, and Per Hansa feels a complete lack of communication with his wife. Beret's moods are mercurial, but Per Hansa tells himself that everything will be all right after she has the baby.

Winter ever tightens its grip. The snows come, and only occasionally does the sun break through. On clear nights the sky is brilliant with stars. Per Hansa worries about Beret but does not know what to do. He frets that the baby has not arrived, and the inactivity of winter bothers him. For a time he thinks of taking a trip to the Souix River to fish through the ice, but realizes that he cannot leave Beret. Instead, he makes her a pair of wooden clogs, and when she tells him he should have made them for her earlier, he is deeply saddened.

One day Henry Solum comes to ask Per Hansa if he will look after their cow for the rest of winter. At first, Per Hansa is pleased, but when he discovers the Solum boys want to leave the cow with him because they are going east for the winter he is furious. Beret remarks that she can understand why the Solum boys want to leave, and this further angers Per Hansa; he says that if they were men instead of worms they would stay on. Subsequently, Per Hansa and Beret have a violent argument, and he leaves the house, works at making skis for himself and the boys, and that evening goes over to Hans Olsa's place. Per Hansa asks Hans Olsa's wife, Sorine, to please go and visit with Beret. Sorine agrees, and tells Per Hansa not to worry.

Shortly after Sorine leaves on her mission, Tonseten turns up and demands to know why Per Handa and Hans Olsa have not tried to stop the Solum boys from leaving. Tonseten suggests they speak to Henry Solum about the possibility of him teaching the children of the settlement. The three men go off to see the Solums. At first the Solums refuse, but after Per Hansa pleads with them, the Solum boys agree to stay if the others' wives will give them a weekly supper and mend their clothes.

The winter days drag on, some sunny, some bleak, but to Beret they are all dark, and she feels that this is God's wrath on her for having married Per Hansa after she had gotten with child out of wedlock. She recalls how her parents had been against the marriage and she is broken-hearted at how she feels she has failed them. At the same time she thinks of the love she had for Per Hansa and the glorious days of their early life together. Beret knows that there is one rival in her affections—Hans Olsa, the one who persuaded Per Hansa to follow him to America. Her parents had pleaded with Per Hansa to stay in Norway but he would have none of it, and Beret recalls how at the time she had gladly gone along with him.

Beret remembers how she had been disappointed when they had first come to America, for there was still poverty even though the rich soil was all around them. She tells herself it is Destiny—the law of life that is punishing her for her sins. No sooner had they reached America than the westward fever had struck the immigrants. While Beret had had no desire to move on Per Hansa had been consumed with ambition for new land, and at the same time he was very tender to her. But Beret feels that Per Hansa will never understand that she cannot be like him.

Beret feels that Destiny has cast her about and finally washed her ashore on the plains. She is convinced that her end is coming and that she will be buried on the Great Plains instead of a churchyard back in Norway. Then she worries about a coffin and decides that her old chest will have to serve the purpose. At the same time she is impressed at Per Hansa's foresight in building the house and stable under one roof, for it is the coziest dwelling in the settlement.

Around Christmas time the women of the settlement take turns being with Beret. On Christmas Eve, Beret takes to her bed and Per Hansa is deeply concerned, especially when Beret tells him she is convinced this is her last day on earth. She begs to be buried in the big chest. Per Hansa tries to comfort her, but she will have none of it. Finally, Per Hansa, in his own agony, tears off into the night and paces back and forth by the hut. Inside, Beret suffers through a difficult delivery, but in time the baby boy does arrive, although Beret still remains distant from Per Hansa.

Sorine tells Per Hansa that the child had been born with the caul and should be christened at once. Per Hansa goes off to get

Hans Olsa to do the job, for he says Hans Olsa is the only man fitted for it. After considerable persuasion, Hans Olsa agrees to do it. Per Hansa says he will name the boy Peder Victorious, a peculiar name for a Norwegian. With the encouragement of his wife, Hans Olsa manages the christening. Afterward, they all have a drink, and realize that it is Christmas.

Commentary

Again, Rolvaag emphasizes the different ways in which Per Hansa and Beret prepare for the coming of winter. Per Hansa is constantly busy, pleased because the net he fashioned has brought them fish and ducks. Beret admits to herself that she is pleased with the whitewashed walls of her sod house that others in the settlement admire, but her state of gloom grows. With the coming of winter Per Hansa is restless because there is little to do, but he does not brood, while Beret sinks deeper and deeper into her dark mood.

Here again, we have the man of action and the woman who thinks of other things than the immediate present. As the mood takes hold of Beret she turns more and more inward, and now she is again beset by the thought of the sin she had committed because she had had relations with Per Hansa before they were legally married.

It should be noted that the Norse people, at least in their literature, are torn by two forces. On the one hand their virile Viking ancestry leads them across the seas — or the plains in this case. On the other, since they were converted to Christianity, they appear to feel a sense of guilt that they had ever been robust pagans. So while they are devout, they still believe in trolls — mystical creatures that did evil and lived in caves in the hills — and their mysticism is not Christian but definitely pagan. Sigrid Undset in *Kristin Lavrandsdatter* draws a somewhat parallel picture to that facing Beret; she also had had an affair with Erland before her marriage, and as time goes by, she is deeply disturbed at what she considers her sinful past. Undset's Nobel Prize winning novel is laid several hundred years before this book, but the heroine's reactions are quite similar to those of Beret's.

The difficult delivery of the child only fortifies Beret's belief that God is punishing her for her sins. And when Per Hansa picks the name Peder Victorious for the newborn boy, she feels he is spitting in the face of providence.

In everything that occurs, Rolvaag is emphasizing the different outlook between men and women. It would be incorrect, probably, to say which sex was the stronger in facing the wilderness, but the outlook was clearly different. And here we have Per Hansa ready to go forward and build his dream empire, especially now that he has another son that he has named the Victorious, while Beret feels that this is another of the follies they have perpetrated in defying the Lord and coming to this desolate land.

BOOK II

CHAPTER I

ON THE BORDER OF UTTER DARKNESS

Summary
The desolation of winter has hit the Great Plains, but the tiny newcomer that Beret brought into the world on Christmas morning makes it less of a burden, for here is the miracle of life. To Beret it is a wonder that she is still alive, and she begins to take a new interest in life. She is troubled, however, that Per Hansa and the boys are not around, but And-Ongen tells her that they are out following wolf tracks. When Per Hansa returns, Beret is happy that she is still alive, and for the next few days she sleeps as she has never slept before, and Per Hansa is kind to her.

The bleakness of the prairie winter continued, but now the folk of the community were able to laugh, for now there was this newcomer among them, and against laughter, what power can prevail? After Beret gets out of bed, she wants to have all the neighbors over for the celebration of the thirteenth day after Christmas, and Per Hansa agrees. The party is a joyous one; all of them feel that they have an interest in the boy that Beret has brought into the world, and they talk of what he may someday become. Finally, Hans Olsa says that the lad may some day be governor, for the prairies will be a state some day. The discussion ends here, but Per Hansa and Beret are happy.

The school that Henry Solum runs becomes a refuge to all of them during the winter and gives them a chance to study English. The school moved from house to house. The school is run on loose lines and in a sense serves as a club. In the beginning Henry Solum does not know what to do, for he has no materials, and resorts to story-telling in Norwegian and English, but in time the men improvise materials so that the children can have something to write upon. They discover that Sam Solum can sing well, and he teaches them many songs.

The bitter winter continues and the settlers begin to run out of fuel, but Hans Olsa discovers that cast-off hay can be twisted into fagots. But in February it becomes necessary for the men to go off to the Sioux River for a further supply of wood. While the others think it is impossible to take oxen on such a journey, Per Hansa is sure that the oxen he has trained to pull a sleigh can make it. The others depend on their horses.

They have to wait for clear weather, but one day they put out in four caravans, Per Hansa bringing up the rear with his slow oxen. Per Hansa's boys are furious at being left behind. Beret sees the caravan off and feels a sense of powerlessness. The caravan moves along in the brilliant sunshine until the middle of the afternoon, but they are then struck by a terrible blizzard.

The storm hits with all its fury and reminds Per Hansa of the many times he has faced them at sea. He drives his team of oxen into the heart of the storm. Per Hansa is freezing, and worries about falling asleep; he thinks of the Rocky Mountains he has heard about and of the Pacific Coast, where there is no winter. Finally, the oxen stop and Per Hansa discovers that they are by a house. He flings open the door and goes in.

Per Hansa is so overcome by the warmth of the room after his ordeal that he has no idea where he is, but he finds out shortly that his companions are there. All of them are together again in the cabin of Simon Baarstad, one of the Norwegian settlers near the Sioux River. Per Hansa is fed, and his spirits return. He jokes about the girl that Sam Solum appears to have found for himself, but later when he tries to sleep he thinks of how Beret must be worrying that night.

Around the area of the Baarstad cabin there was quite a settlement of Norwegians from the Tronder area. They had been there for a good many years and were well settled. For two days the men from the settlement cut wood, and the Tronders show them great hospitality. Before they leave, they order wheat and oats from the Tronders, and Tonseten even buys a sack of barley in order to brew beer. Per Hansa goes fishing through the ice on the river and that night they all eat fish. Later, there is a dance among the settlers and it is obvious to Per Hansa that Sam Solum is very close to the Baarstad girl. The next morning, before daylight, the men leave the settlement and are on their way back to Spring Creek.

On a Sunday afternoon the whole settlement is gathered in Tonseten's hut; a gloomy restlessness has taken hold of all of them as the winter continues. The courage of the men is slowly ebbing away, but they talk hopefully of the day that this land will be filled with settlers. Suddenly, Tonseten asks them what names they intend to use when they take out the title deeds to their lands. They are all surprised but discuss the matter. Beret is the only one that does not join in the hilarity while they joke about the new "American" names they may take. Per Hansa decides that he will call himself Holm, and Hans Olsa settles on Vaag. But Beret stays awake late that night, thinking of how they are now even discarding the names of their ancestors, and she is unhappy. The old fear that she is going crazy comes back to her; a dark cloud hangs over her and she cannot rid herself of it.

In March, Per Hansa achieves something that is still told about in the legends of the settlement. He had heard from the Tronders at Sioux River about Indians at Flandreau who trapped all winter and sold muskrat, among other animals, for a fifth of the price the furs would bring in Minnesota. He determines to buy a supply of furs

from the Indians and transport them east for sale, but he is short
of funds and realizes he must bring the rest of the settlement into
the venture. Beret is very troubled when he tells her that he will
have to leave her alone for some time, but Per Hansa says that he
must go if they are to have clothes for the children and other much
needed things. Ultimately, Per Hansa goes alone and reaches Flandreau the first night, riding his pony. He bargains with the Indians
and they sell him furs which he loads on the pony and takes into Minnesota. He is gone a week, and then he goes off again. In all, he makes
three journeys, and finally is able to show Beret $140 that he has
made. In addition he brings back many things for the house. But all
through this endeavor Per Hansa is disturbed, for Beret does not
share in his excitement.

Commentary

This chapter of Book II is concerned with the winter that the
settlers are facing, but it is again a story of the indomitable Per
Hansa to whom everything is a challenge to be met and beaten.

In the beginning, we find that Beret is happier than she has been
because she now has the new baby, and the community shares her
happiness. But Beret has not adjusted to life in the wilderness, and
she never will.

It is always Per Hansa who adjusts to this new environment: he
is the one who makes faggots out of cast-off hay, who uses oxen to
go and fetch wood while the others rely on the faster but less durable
horses, and who finally thinks of selling furs trapped by Indians
and thus get some cash. He is, we gather, always cheerful and indus-
trious, while Beret is again beset by fears. Per Hansa feels he is
accomplishing something, but he and Beret are moving further apart,
and this is the one thing that disturbs the man of action. He can cope
with the bleak land and the elements but not with the unhappy
woman that he loves.

CHAPTER II

THE POWER OF EVIL IN HIGH PLACES

Summary

Per Hansa and the boys sit around the table in their hut sifting the seed wheat he has gotten from the Tronders, and Per Hansa realizes how important this task is, for it means food and money for his family. After the work on the seed is done and spring finally arrives, Per Hansa is impatient to begin plowing but the ground is still too wet. In the middle of April Per Hansa decides the ground is dry enough and begins the plowing and seeding. Per Hansa is delighted to be seeding his own land, but in the afternoon Tonseten comes over and tells him he is crazy to sow so soon. But Per Hansa is happy, and the next day he and the boys finish the job.

The day after the seeding it starts to rain, and then to snow, and Per Hansa is broken-hearted at the thought of what may happen to his wheat. He is like a sick man broken in spirit. Soon the sun comes out and the snow melts, but all Per Hansa can think of is the precious seed wheat he wasted. When spring is fully on them Tonseten begins his seeding and Per Hansa watches him and thinks of what a fool he had been to try and buck the seasons. He goes to his field, digs up two kernels and feels the devil has cursed him for his folly.

The two boys work on four acres that Per Hansa had broken earlier and suggest to their father that they plant potatoes. Per Hansa is still very unhappy but realizes this may be the only thing to do. For the rest of the week Per Hansa and the boys plant potatoes. On Sunday, Per Hansa thinks of going to the Sioux River again and try to get some seed wheat, but at this moment the boys burst into the hut to say that the wheat is sprouting. Per Hansa rushes out and sees his field is full of green shoots. It is emotionally almost too much for Per Hansa and he cries softly. When he returns home, the spring is in his step again.

As the spring wore on the Irish arrived and took up homesteads near the sloughs; later, other Norwegian settlers arrived. The boy, Hans, and the son of an allegedly wealthy newcomer get into a fight over Hans' pony, the one that Per Hansa received from the Indian chief. The boys fight but eventually make up. The new boy's father has large plans for his land. He comes over one day to hire Per Hansa to help in building a house. The man, Torkel Tallaksen, speaks grandly of the things he intends to do and shows his contempt for Per Hansa's sod hut. Per Hansa tells Tallaksen that he has things twisted around, and had better start with essentials rather than building at this moment. But Beret is impressed and tells Tallaksen that his wife must be glad that he intends to build a decent house in this wilderness. Tallaksen's plans go awry when he cannot get men to do his work, and by fall another sod hut was built.

That summer many caravans passed through the settlement on their way west. They were people of many nationalities and seemed strange to the settlement, and they would not stop but rolled on westward. But one day a single wagon, with two cows following behind, stops at Per Hansa's hut. The immigrants are Norwegians, a couple with three young children. The wife is evidently insane, for she has been tied to a chest in the wagon. Beret feels an immediate sympathy for the woman and tries to help her. Per Hansa talks with the man and decides he is a drifter. The man tells Per Hansa a sad story of their trip and of the death on the prairie of their youngest boy. When Per Hansa and the man go into the hut they discover that Beret has put the woman in bed and she is asleep. Later Beret tells Per Hansa that this experience only fortifies her belief that life on the prairie is impossible.

The strange woman remembers how she felt when she was first brought into the hut by Beret, and how good it was to be looked after and put to bed. Later, she awakens and on a crazy impulse snatches the little girl And-Ongen and runs off into the night. Beret awakens and realizes what has happened. She and Per Hansa frantically begin the search, and find the woman on top of the hill, And-Ongen asleep in her arms. The woman is obsessed by the thought of her boy buried out on the prairie, but she is touched when Per Hansa and Hans Olsa make a coffin for her boy and go off to find where he is buried. The men are gone for four days but find nothing.

After the return from the search for the boy's grave, the strangers go west again. Per Hansa is appalled at the lack of planning on the man's part, but says nothing. Beret is deeply troubled that she did not do more for the strangers. Per Hansa and the boys are hard at work plowing, but Beret feels only a sense of horrible lonesomeness. After supper they are planning to meet Hans Olsa to talk about a trip into town, but Beret is unable to shake her mood of deep depression. She feels an evil power has been let loose among them in this terrible wilderness. To shut out the prairie, she covers the windows, and when Per Hansa and the boys return in high spirits, she will have nothing to do with him. As the days go by, Beret feels the evil spirit is always with her. At first, Per Hansa teases her about it, but after a while he is affected by her fears.

As July arrives the wheat slowly ripens, promising a rich harvest. Per Hansa is pleased with his fields but worried about how Beret feels, and wonders what he can do to cheer her up. Per Hansa has the finest field of wheat in the area and his neighbors come to marvel at it. His potatoes are growing well, too, and he is generous in giving them to the newly-settled Irish. Per Hansa is filled with pride, and when Tonseten tells him it is time to harvest he says he will hold off a while longer. Tonseten is the reaper for the settlement and he finally insists he must start on Per Hansa's land. The harvesting starts and the whole settlement watches. After sundown they stop for the day and go to Per Hansa's for supper, and everyone is joyous.

The next day the harvesting is completed and Tonseten feels proud that he has proved his prowess to his neighbors. As for the four acres of oats that Per Hansa had planted, Tonseten says it will be child's play. Per Hansa, Tonseten, and Hans Olsa are all pleased, until Per Hansa notices an ominous cloud formation in the west. In no time at all the storm is upon them, but it is not nature's storm, but a sky full of locusts. The grasshoppers drop down and devour everything in sight while the people of the settlement look on helplessly. They talk of the plagues in scripture until finally Henry Solum brings them back to reality and insists they try to harvest all they can. Per Hansa gets his old muzzle-loader and fires into the flock. This drives them off his land, but the locusts go on to the other fields in the settlement. But the men are stirred to activity and by nightfall finish Per Hansa's oat field; they are gnawed by anxiety and want to start harvesting their own fields even though the wheat may not be quite ripe yet. The others go off and Per Hansa walks home, bothered in mind because he has not seen Beret all day and feels that something is wrong. When he reaches the hut the door is shut. He shouts for Beret to open it but she will not. Per Hansa is forced to shove it open. Inside it is pitch black and Beret is inside the big chest with the baby in her arms and the little girl And-Ongen at her feet. Per Hansa is horrified. Beret asks him why the devil has not got him yet; she says he has been around all afternoon. Per Hansa's agony at seeing his wife in this state is too much for him and he faints.

The plague of grasshoppers continues through the years from 1873 to part of 1878, then disappears as mysteriously as it had come. Some of the settlers were wiped out but most of them hung on grimly, although they knew the locusts would come again. In the meanwhile, new settlers, drawn by the rich soil, arrive and take up homesteads. Beset by the locusts, the people could only put their faith in God.

Commentary

This chapter is still the saga of Per Hansa, the man of action, and of how good luck accompanies his efforts because he is not afraid to fight his battle against any odds. First, there is what seems to be the tragedy of planting the wheat too soon, but presently this becomes a blessing.

Despite his physical triumphs, however, Per Hansa cannot conquer Beret's fears; she, in her own way, continues to fight, but her fight is against the wilderness—a negative one that she does not wish to win but wants to run away from.

Rolvaag now prepares us for what is to come by introducing the drifting Norwegian settler and his crazed wife. Beret feels an immediate sympathy for the woman who has lost her mind over the grief of losing her son. Per Hansa's reaction is disgust at the drifter's lack of planning, and he reacts to the visit by getting his friend Hans Olsa to accompany him to try and find the dead child's grave. This is a positive action, but in the meanwhile Beret comforts the sick woman and is further convinced that the Great Plains are no place for civilized people to live. We are led to believe that more-and-more, Per Hansa and Beret are being drawn apart, and Per Hansa is unable to do anything to prevent the schism in their relationship.

Now for the first time a physical act over which Per Hansa has no control strikes him. While — because of his luck — he is not overly affected, the settlement is literally wiped out by the invasion of the locusts. Now Beret is, in a sense, the winner in the conflict of wills. The visitation of the trolls or of the devil that she has feared all along has come to pass, and she is the victor over Per Hansa who all along has felt that with courage and determination the wilderness could be conquered. Up to this moment he had proved this, but now he is helpless in the face of the plague. Beret is triumphant, but at the cost of her own reason.

CHAPTER III

THE GLORY OF THE LORD

Summary

One day in June a man driving a dilapidated cart turns up at the settlement and is met by Tonseten. It turns out that the stranger is a minister. The Tonsetens bring out the best things they have to eat and entertain the minister.

The minister smokes his pipe and talks on into the night with Tonseten and Kjersti and finally is shown to bed in the spare sod hut. Tonseten is desirous of having a private talk with the minister but cannot do so while his wife is still awake. Tonseten has something to reveal to the minister that has been torturing him for a long time: as the elected justice of the peace of the area he had illegally in the eyes of God, in Tonseten's view, married a young couple who now had several children. In the morning the minister asks detailed questions about the people living in the area. The minister tells Tonseten to get the people together and he will conduct divine services that afternoon. It is decided to hold them at Per Hansa's. Tonseten tells the minister how Per Hansa has prospered but that his wife, Beret, is sorely tried. On the way to Per Hansa's, Tonseten tells the minister about the marriage ceremony he had performed. The minister tells Tonseten that it was unusual but legal and perfectly justified under the circumstances. Tonseten is relieved and overjoyed.

The minister holds a service at Per Hansa's, and the people of the community are much impressed; he speaks of the privations of the tribes of Israel and compares it to the life of the pioneers on the plains. But, he says, they are founding a kingdom. Tonseten is particularly pleased, and feels that so long as he had done no wrong in the past in marrying a couple, there is no reason he should not serve the minister as a sexton. The minister baptizes several children, including Per Hansa and Beret's latest son, the Victorious. But as the minister is about to perform the ceremony, Beret breaks down and cries that no child can be called that in this wilderness. Per Hansa manages to calm her down but Beret has been like a mad woman.

After the ceremony the people remain in the yard for a time, talking about the sermon and about the tragedy of Beret. Inside the house the minister stays with a few of the women. He suggests that they go home but that one remain to help Beret and that they come often to visit, but singly. The minister then takes the child and goes out to the yard and tells the people to go home and pray. After a while the minister notices sounds from the stable; when he gets there he sees Beret and Per Hansa seated on a bale of hay. The minister asks if he may stay for supper and Beret goes off to prepare it, while the minister stays in the stable with Per Hansa and asks him to tell the story of what has happened to Beret. Per Hansa tells the tale of how he was the one who wished to go west against Beret's wishes and of how they had slept together before they were married. He asks the minister what he is now supposed to do when his beloved wife seems to be losing her mind? The minister tells him to trust in God, but Per Hansa rejects this and they have an argument. After a while both men calm down and Per Hansa says it was wrong of him to bring Beret to this wilderness and finally to name the last born "Victorious." The minister says he does not agree—that it is a wonderful name, and he cannot understand why Beret objects to it. The minister then asks when Beret began to have these attacks and Per Hansa tells him it started with the coming of the grasshoppers, and of how Beret might have harmed the child had not Sorine been with her, and of other acts of madness. The minister tries to comfort Per Hansa and asks that he have a chance to talk with Beret alone the next day. As the two men return to the hut Ole comes running to say that Hans is sitting by the Indian mound crying because he is afraid of his mother. Per Hansa goes off into the night and the minister enters the hut. Per Hansa finds Hans and consoles him, then leads him home.

Beret and Sorine are in the hut when the minister enters, and everything is calm. Later, Per Hansa arrives with the boys, and when the minister sees by his swollen face that Hans has been crying, he is troubled and begins to pray. The others join him, and there is a strange peace in the hut. After a time the minister blesses the child he had christened earlier and calls upon him to "become a true victor here." Beret is confused and messes up the sewing she had been working on. The next morning the minister is cheerful and hungry. After Per Hansa and boys go out he talks with Beret and tells her he expects to hold a Communion Service in the hut within two weeks. Beret is astonished, but at the same time comforted, and after the minister leaves she is very gentle to the little boy.

During the summer of 1877 a great many wagons came across the prairie. Some go further west but others settle in the area. The grasshopper plague is still on them, but the farmers manage to salvage something; the livestock and poultry holdings continue to grow. And then the railroad came as far as Luverne and it looks as though before long it will reach Sioux Falls. That summer, a number of houses, including Hans Olsa's, went up in the settlement. The trees that had been planted on the barren plains also flourished.

The weather is beautiful on the day of the Communion and many people from the various communities in the area are on hand. The minister is sorely troubled because he does not feel that the Lord has given him the faith he needs to comfort these folk in the wilderness. But he goes through the Communion and feels that possibly he has brought something to the people who have taken part in it. The minister is troubled, and feels that he is not fulfilling his part, but carries on, and in the end tells a very commonplace story instead of giving a sermon. After the Communion the minister gets in his ancient cart and leaves, saying he will be back in a month. He feels that he has completely failed the people.

Now the time has come when Hans Olsa builds himself a real house and not just a sod hut. He and Sorine have some arguments about its arrangements but in the end Hans Olsa gives in, for he has learned that Sorine is pregnant. Things have been going well for Hans Olsa, but he is worried about Beret and Per Hansa, for he has seen what Beret's madness has done to their life. He asks his wife if they should offer to take the little boy and bring him up, but Sorine says that while she has no objection, she doubts if it will be possible.

Beret sits in the old sod barn that Per Hansa long since had made over into a workshop and storehouse, and sews a shirt for her baby, while Per Hansa repairs the roof of the new barn. She thinks of how Per Hansa can manage his work but of how lost she is. At the same time she remembers the minister and how he had relieved her from so many of her burdens, and she daydreams of her son becoming a minister himself. Beret imagines that her mother will be coming from Norway and she can tell her that her grandson will become a minister. She is brought out of her reverie by the arrival of Hans Olsa, and hears him talking to Per Hansa about taking the child if she were to have another spell. She hears Per Hansa say that it is not possible, that she needs the child with her and that it has been his fault in bringing her to this wilderness. Beret is happy at what Per Hansa has said, and she listens no more. She goes into the house and showers her affection on the little boy.

As she plays with the little boy, Beret feels drowsy, and in time she sleeps. When she awakes, she is struck with wonder at where she is, and feels she has been away a long time. She gets food for the child, but has to search for things. She is overjoyed at a thought of returning home. When she finally sees Per Hansa he looks at her as though she were some stranger, and when she gets hot milk for him, he is unable to speak to her. Beret is worried that Per Hansa has a cold and insists that he go to bed; but Per Hansa gets up quickly and plays boisterously with the little boy. Beret looks on, smiling.

Commentary

The coming of the itinerant minister to the settlement is significant in showing the deep religious faith of the pioneers in the wilderness. Here again, however, the individuals act differently to the ministrations of the man of God. Tonseten, the weak man among the first group, is delighted because the minister assures him that he has committed no sin in marrying a couple in his capacity as justice of the peace.

Per Hansa is pleased that the minister sees no wrong in naming his son "Victorious," but his need for the minister is minimal. On the other hand Beret is comforted by his visit and seems to feel a ray of hope. But in the final analysis, it is not the minister, but Per Hansa who unconsciously brings Beret out of her madness, for when she overhears Per Hansa talking with Hans Olsa about the possibility of the latter taking over the care of her little boy, and by the conversation realizes how deeply her husband loves her she once again becomes a woman.

The point should perhaps not be over-emphasized, but here again Rolvaag brings out the different approach Per Hansa and Beret have to problems. The man of action, the good man Per Hansa, does not need spiritual comfort; he is strong in his own convictions. On the other hand the sensitive Beret needs a crutch. She finds some of it with the minister, but ultimately what saves her is her knowledge that she is dearly loved.

CHAPTER IV

THE GREAT PLAIN DRINKS THE BLOOD OF CHRISTIAN MEN AND IS SATISFIED

Summary
Many were the tales told of the pioneers on the Great Plains, of the years of travail, of how some could not stand it and went mad. All the forces of nature seemed to be turned against the settlers. But the people kept coming and they felt that nothing was impossible.

During the winter of 1880-81 it snowed 40 days twice, from the middle of October until April, and seldom ceased. The suffering was great, for all kinds of supplies gave out. One settler, Torkel

Tallaksen, ground his own flour, and borrowed coffee grinders from his neighbors. When his son is returning Tonseten's mill, he falls in a snowdrift and loses it. The greatest tragedy was the lack of fuel. Whole herds of cattle died that winter, and many people, too.

Hans Olsa had acquired a large herd of cattle, and had managed to keep them well fed into February, and figured the winter would surely be over soon. On the 7th of February a snowstorm came up and Hans Olsa thought it best to go out and look after the cattle. He finds that the shed he had built for them is in bad shape and that the cattle will not survive unless he can repair it at once. He gets to work and manages to patch it up, but it is night by then and he has a hard time driving the cattle into the shed. Hans Olsa is exhausted by this time and realizes he cannot find his way home in the dark and the storm, and he decides to stay with the animals. Then he notices that he is frost-bitten and must get to a house or will be dead by morning. With an effort of will he starts off into the night.

Hans Olsa staggers into his house in the early hours of the morning, too exhausted even to take off his clothes. Sorine tries everything she can to help him, but Hans Olsa is now a very sick man. For two days the blizzard rages, but when it abates, Hans Olsa tells his daughter, Sofie, to go and get Per Hansa. Per Hansa decides that they must get help from an Irish woman who had settled nearby and is known for her healing knowledge. Per Hansa goes to fetch "Crazy Bridget." The old woman prepares poultices to put on Hans Olsa. Per Hansa goes off to look after Hans Olsa's cattle and to do necessary chores at his own place. In the evening Tonseten drops by and when Per Hansa tells him the news he goes off to see Hans Olsa and is troubled. Tonseten tries to be cheerful but fears the worst.

Beret, who has come to Hans Olsa's, is disgusted because Tonseten, in her opinion, is unseemly in the presence of death. Beret sits by Hans Olsa's bed, and when he awakens after a fit of coughing she tells him he should prepare himself for the afterlife. But Hans Olsa is not quite ready to die yet, and does not take kindly to the suggestion. Beret thinks of how she and Hans Olsa grew up together in Norway, and she is grieved to think she will not see him after death because he will die before receiving Holy Communion. Hans

Olsa asks if it might be possible to get him a doctor, but Beret is more interested in getting him a minister. Beret kneels by the bed and prays. At dawn a settler comes and pleads for Beret to come with him because his wife is expecting a baby. Beret reluctantly goes with him.

Later, Per Hansa drops into Hans Olsa's to see how things are going and arranges with the Solum boys to look after the herd. The people of the settlement are hard at work now that the storm is over, and they help each other in any way they can. Hans Olsa's condition is serious, and he asks Per Hansa to stay with him. Hans Olsa awakens late at night and tells Per Hansa what he wants done after his death; he asks Per Hansa to take on various responsibilities for his family. Per Hansa feels that Hans Olsa wants to tell him something else, and eventually realizes that Hans Olsa wants a minister but is reluctant to ask him to go for one because of the weather.

All through the summer and into early fall Per Hansa had driven himself and the boys. He was happy that Beret was better and did not worry about her growing religious concern; he looked upon her still as a frail child. However, shortly before Christmas they had a falling out over the subject of daily devotions, and Per Hansa was not pleased at how Beret spoke of him as a sinner in her prayers.

At dawn Per Hansa returns from the bedside of Hans Olsa and says that someone must go for the minister. Beret tells him he must go, for unless the minister comes Hans Olsa will die in sin. Per Hansa says that if this is so, Hans Olsa will have a lot going along from the settlement. Per Hansa goes on to say that with the weather as it is, it would be impossible for anyone to cross the prairie, but Beret keeps after him. Per Hansa storms out of the house, furious that grown people — Hans Olsa and Beret — are acting so stupidly. Later, he goes with the boys to look after Hans Olsa's cattle, and he feels a little better, but when he goes home he finds Sorine there, and she tells him that the Irish woman Bridget had been to see Hans Olsa and had said that there was no hope of recovery. Sorine says that she realizes it is impossible to travel anywhere, but she implies that Per Hansa should try. After supper, Beret says she is going to Henry Solum to try and get him to fetch the minister for Hans Olsa. Per Hansa flies into a rage, tells her to stay in the house, and leaves.

Per Hansa is in a rage, but cools down quickly. He puts on his skis and goes off to see two men who had settled in the district recently and are expert skismiths. Meanwhile, Beret is agitated because she now realizes she has said too much. In about an hour Per Hansa returns with two pairs of skis. He says goodbye to the boys, who are playing, and pay little attention to their father. As Per Hansa leaves he thinks that he sees Beret looking after him from a window. He pushes westward although it is a test of will not to turn back. Beret rushes out of the house and calls to Per Hansa, but he has gone beyond the range of her voice. Per Hansa drops in at Hans Olsa's and talks for a while; he says he is going for the minister and Hans Olsa is tearfully grateful. Per Hansa straps on his skis and starts off into the storm. His thoughts are of home, of Beret and the children. He pushes on as darkness falls.

One day in the spring after Hans Olsa had died, some boys come across a haystack. Sitting with his back to the mouldering hay is a man, one pair of skis beside him and the other pair strapped to his back. "To the boys it looked as though the man were sitting there resting while he waited for better skiing....His face was ashen and drawn. His eyes were set toward the west."

Commentary

As we come to the end of the book man is still fighting the elements; the grasshoppers are gone but now the terrible winter has come.

Per Hansa and Hans Olsa, the strong ones in the settlement, have been doing well, but now Hans Olsa is struck down and the only man of action left is Per Hansa. We gather that while he feels deep sympathy for his old friend, his concern is for Hans Olsa's physical rather than spiritual being. But on all sides—and even from Hans Olsa himself—he is beset by those who consider Hans Olsa's spiritual welfare more important. Beret, as her former actions have shown, is obsessed by the idea that Hans Olsa will die in "sin." Per Hansa is infuriated by this statement, for he considers his best friend the finest of men, but when he finds that Hans Olsa himself is deeply troubled at facing death without religious ministration he makes the decision to go for the minister although it is obvious that the weather makes it an almost impossible undertaking.

Beret, in her insistence that Per Hansa should go for the minister even though he tells her it is impossible, is a rather unsympathetic character. It is only after Per Hansa leaves that she apparently has a change of mind and heart. When she rushes out into the blizzard to call him back, we are led to believe that she now realizes what she may be losing. But it is too late, just as it is too late for the boys to say a fond goodbye to their beloved father.

Per Hansa dies alone — very much alone — and the tragedy is complete. The indomitable man has been ground down by fate.

GENERAL COMMENT

Basically, this is a strange book, for it was written by one who is European in background but writes about America — an America to which he was an immigrant like the characters in this book. His aim is obviously to tell about the contributions that the Norwegians made to the building of their adopted land, and in this he succeeds admirably.

However, despite the fact that the scene is America, the story is not. The author is primarily interested in psychology and not in plotting. The story is of pioneers on the Great Plains and of the physical conditions they are forced to conquer, but behind it all, Rolvaag is more interested in what the pioneering meant in terms of mental anguish rather than in the basic facts of the difficulty of carving a home out of the wilderness.

Per Hansa is the true pioneer, the man of strength and pragmatism. To him, the prairie is a challenge to be met with whatever weapons he has at his command. In this he is as successful as any can be, but he is not concerned with the deeper meanings of coming to an unknown land. On the other hand, his wife Beret is tormented by being torn away from all that she was familiar with, and is in a sense a failure as a pioneer wife. Fittingly, if we consider the rather gloomy Norse philosophy, it is she that drives her husband off into the blizzard so that the ancient gods may be appeased and the great prairie satisfied. This is not an unusual theme in Norse literature, although perhaps not in this exact context.

Many observers have commented on the strange seeming contradiction of a Norwegian writing a great American novel. But one should keep in mind that this is a novel about an aspect of American life and American history, and while it was originally written in Norwegian it is about Norwegian-Americans and told by one who should know more about them than, let us say, an Irish-American.

This is not the only novel that has been written about the early settlers on the great plains. The great American woman writer, Willa Cather, turned out a novel about settlers on the Great Plains called *O Pioneers!* that told somewhat the same story as this one, but was laid in Nebraska.

The question is asked by critics whether *Giants in the Earth* should be regarded as a work of Norwegian literature or American literature. The question would seem to be academic. This is a work by a Norwegian-American about America.

ANALYSIS OF MAIN CHARACTERS

Per Hansa

The male protagonist of this novel is the true pioneer, the man of action. To him, the prairie is something to be conquered by work, and more work. While he loves his wife and children, he is fundamentally interested in what he can do with the virgin soil of this new land, for the land-hunger of the European peasant is strong in him. He is a strong man, both physically and spiritually, and he is above all an optimist who believes that so long as he labors hard enough in this new world, all things will come to his beloved family. He is also an inventive man—the duck nets—the sod-house-barn combination are notable examples of his inventiveness. He is also a shrewd man, well suited to the frontier life, and except for the setbacks from nature, one who loves the life. We are not told too much about his past in Norway, but it is clear that at one time he was a fisherman in the Lofoten Islands. This fishing area, where cod and herring abound, is located above the Artic Circle, and the fishermen must perforce be a very hardy lot. Per Hansa and his best friend, Hans Olsa, are just that. And yet both of them are finally destroyed by the elements. In the words of Ernest Hemingway: "The world breaks every one and afterward many are strong at the broken places. But those that will not break it kills." Per Hansa is one that will not break. The irony of his end is that he takes off on his last journey against his best judgment only to please his wife and best friend, and we can deduce that he feels the undertaking is hopeless. Per Hansa is overall an admirable character, although perhaps not one that a sensitive person would like; his final act is one of the highest heroism — and it is as always a physical one.

Beret

Per Hansa's wife is the complete antithesis of her husband. She feels that she has sinned through her love of Per Hansa, and in the long brooding hours on the Dakota plains her mind gives way. She cannot share in Per Hansa's delight in the newborn son, Peder Victorious — symbol of Per Hansa's faith in his new environment. Beret sees nothing but devils and trolls around her, and every minute on the frontier is an ordeal. True, she is a woman, and the lot of a frontier life was a hard one, but Beret made it harder by her brooding introspective nature, her sense of sin and her hunger for the Norway that she had left to follow her husband to a new land. Rolvaag's protrayal of this tortured woman is a masterful study into the deep recesses of the soul. The reader at first glance will not find Beret a sympathetic character, but a further study will reveal that she is truly a tragic character and more to be sympathized with than castigated. In the end she destroys unknowingly the one thing she loves dearly — her husband. We are not told what happens after Per Hansa's death, but one can only imagine that Beret will again descend into her dark world of despair.

Hans Olsa

The giant that is Per Hansa's best friend is also a true pioneer, but lacking the imagination and incentive of his comrade. He has also been a Lofoten Island fisherman, and physically he is every bit a match for Per Hansa, and yet, we gather that he lacks the drive of the latter. Materially, he is the best off of the settlers, and this is possibly one reason why he does not try as hard. Also, towards the end of the book, he loses his pragmatic outlook and longs for spiritual comfort, to a point where he is willing to sacrifice his best friend in order to try and find it. There is nothing weak about Hans Olsa, and he is a true pioneer, but he is not in a class with Per Hansa.

Sorine

Hans Olsa's wife, differing from Beret, is the kindly, bovine type that can take any way of life so long as she is with her husband. While she may not be happy in the wilderness, it is enough for her that she is maintaining a household.

Tonseten

Syvert is a rather complicated character. While on the surface he is a weakling, clinging to his wife Kjersti for comfort, and on his friends Per Hansa and Hans Olsa for physical help, he is nonetheless a man of some conviction and courage. The very fact that he is on the prairie is proof of this. He is also a man of considerable ingenuity and knowledge, as attested to by his ability to reap and to brew beer. Tonseten seems to realize his own weaknesses, but tries to bluff his way through life.

The Minister

A wandering Norwegian minister, who is apparently a Calvinist, he is never identified by name. Rolvaag depicts him as a rather complex character, who on one hand is a fundamentalist out to save souls, and on the other a very human and sympathetic character. His understanding of Beret's problem, and of the deep sorrow this brings to Per Hansa is a very touching thing. The minister is a real man of God, in the best sense of the word.

STYLE

In any discussion of Rolvaag's style of writing, it must be remembered that he wrote in Norwegian, his native language, and that this—his classic work—is a translation into English. While a good translator can presumably bring out a great many elements of the original, a critical analysis of the style of a translation is obviously impossible unless the critic is versed in the language of the original version, and even then, it would seem that the criticism would be of the translation rather than of the style of writing.

In this English translation — in which Rolvaag himself assisted — it would seem that he wrote tersely and without unnecessary embellishment. Again, one is reminded of Knut Hamsun's novels, which in their English translations at least, are masterpieces of simple writing. On the other hand, Sigrid Undset's Nobel Prize winning *Kristin Lavransdatter* — again in its English translation — is far more complex.

Suffice to say, this novel has few frostings on the cake of the story. It is told in a forthright way, which fits in admirably with the mood and the locale of the story.

QUESTIONS AND SUGGESTIONS FOR THEMES

BOOK I

1. Who was in the caravan of Per Hansa? Where were they heading? Did Per Hansa have to move into the wilderness? Write a theme on what you think motivated Per Hansa to move westward.

2. Who was already at the settlement when Per Hansa arrived? What did the settlers build their huts out of? What is the trouble with Beret, according to Hans Olsa? Write a theme on your impression of the early days of the settlement on the Great Plains.

3. What do the families eat when Per Hansa and Beret arrive at the settlement? What is the main thing that bothers Beret at this stage? How much land did the settlers receive from the government? Write a theme on what you think Per Hansa believes he can do with his new lands.

4. What is the first crop that Per Hansa plants? What seeds had Beret brought with her? What was the difference between Per Hansa's sod hut and that of the others in the settlement? Write a theme on your impression of the hopes of these early settlers before they are forced to face the winter that is soon coming.

5. What was as "rare as gold?" What were the women's outlets in times of stress? Write a theme on what you think were the main fears of the pioneers at this time.

6. What is Per Hansa's attitude when the Indian train comes? Beret's? Sam Solum's? What is it that Per Hansa gets from the Indians on his first visit to their camp? Write a theme on your impression of these wandering Indians.

7. In what way was the sick Indian hurt? Where had Per Hansa gained his crude medical experience? What is the Norwegian "horse cure?" What do the Indians give Per Hansa? Write a theme on the background of Per Hansa and Hans Olsa in Norway.

8. What happened to the cows? What are Beret's fears at this time? Write a theme on the difference between Per Hansa's and Beret's attitudes after the cows disappear.

9. How many acres did Per Hansa work? What was it that irked Per Hansa about the Sabbath? Write a theme on the dream that Per Hansa has for the future.

10. What is it that the boys find? What is it that Per Hansa finds? Write a theme on your impression of homesteading at this time.

11. What was the crime that Beret felt Per Hansa had committed? What is the first commercial transaction that takes place in the settlement? Write a theme on your impression of the Irish settlers.

12. What was it about Hans Olsa that made "strangers stop and look?" What is Per Hansa's plan that Tonseten objects to? Write a theme on why you think there were land jumpers at a time when land was plentiful on the Great Plains.

13. What was the memorable event that stirred the settlement? What was the name of the town to which the railroad was coming? Write a theme on why the Norwegians in the settlement were so eager to have others settle in the area.

14. How did Per Hansa get his cash supply? What does Per Hansa give the Halling family on his way into Worthington? What are the various things that Per Hansa trades for? Write a theme on your impression of Per Hansa at this period.

15. What is it that the boys fight over? What is the meat that Beret gets from Tonseten? Write a theme on your impression of Beret's continuing depression.

16. How does Beret resolve to get back to "civilization?" What is Per Hansa's reaction when he is told about the badger? Write a theme about what you feel is happening to Beret.

17. What is it that Per Hansa is so proud of in the sod hut? Why is Per Hansa happy that the snow has come? Write a theme on the difference of how Per Hansa, Hans Olsa, and Beret face the desolation of the plains.

18. Why does Per Hansa feel so contented when winter comes? What changes his mood? On what do the Norwegians blame the weather? Write a theme on your impression of the first winter.

19. What makes Per Hansa furious? What is Tonseten's idea? What is the proposition the Solum boys make? Write a theme on Beret's "sin."

20. What was the "plague" that hit the early settlements? What is the end of life as Beret envisages it? Write a theme on the spirit of the community in time of crisis.

21. What is so unusual about the new baby? Who Christens the baby? Write a theme on the religious belief of the settlers.

QUESTIONS AND SUGGESTIONS FOR THEMES

BOOK II

1. What is the factor that gives the settlers new hope the first winter? What is the name Per Hansa picks for his child? Write a theme on what the Solum boys' school means to the settlers.

2. What is the new fuel that Hans Olsa discovers? What is different about Per Hansa's sled? What happens to Per Hansa in the blizzard? Write a theme about the fuel gathering trip of the settlers.

3. Who are the settlers along the Sioux River? What are the stories they relate? Write a theme comparing these Sioux River pioneers with the characters in the book.

4. What purchase from the Tronders does Tonseten conceal from his comrades? Who is it that Sam Solum has at the dance? Write a theme on your impression of this pioneer party.

5. What is the question of names that Tonseten initiates? What name does Per Hansa pick for himself? Write a theme on this matter of Norwegian names.

6. What is the enterprise that Per Hansa attempts with the Indians? What is the result? Write a theme on the different manner in which Per Hansa and Beret view the venture.

7. What does Per Hansa consider the most important task with the seed wheat? Why do the others in the settlement disagree

with Per Hansa's timing on planting seed? Write a theme on what you think of Per Hansa's experiment.

8. What brings on Per Hansa's deep depression? What do the boys suggest they plant? Write a theme on why wheat is considered so important by the settlers.

9. Who is the "rich" settler who comes in the summer? What is it about his ambitions that impresses Beret? Write a theme on what you think of this "rich" settler's ideas.

10. Who are the Norwegians that arrive in the old wagon? What is wrong with the woman? Write a theme on the impression this family makes on Beret.

11. What is it that this family left on the Great Plains? What does the strange woman do that upsets them all? Write a theme on the difference between Per Hansa and this wandering settler.

12. What is it about Beret's actions that saddens Per Hansa? How is the crop doing? Write a theme on the settlers' feelings about the first harvesting of wheat.

13. What does Tonseten feel about the harvest? What do the settlers think the "storm" is at first? How does Per Hansa drive the grasshoppers from his fields? Write a theme on what you know of locust swarms and what they do to vegetation.

14. What does the grasshopper invasion do to Beret? What does it do to the settlers? Write a theme on your impression of the fortitude of the pioneers.

15. Who is the lone man that comes in the old cart? Why is Tonseten so glad to see him? Write a theme on your impression of this stranger.

16. What does Tonseten wish to speak to the minister about? Why is Tonseten's conscience bothering him? Write a theme on your impression of Tonseten as revealed in this chapter.

17. Where does the minister hold the meeting? What does the minister preach about? Write a theme on what you think the coming of the minister means to the settlers.

18. What does the minister suggest that the people do in regard to Beret? What is the tragedy the minister senses? What does Per Hansa tell the minister about Beret? What happens to Hans, and why? Write a theme on Beret's sickness.

19. Why is the minister unable to eat the dinner that Beret prepares? What does the minister say about the little baby? Write a theme on what impression you think the minister made on Beret.

20. What happened in the summer and fall of '77? What was the monster that the settlers welcomed? Write a theme on the growth of the settlements on the Great Plains.

21. What is the service the minister intends to give? What does the minister feel is lacking in him? Write a theme on the minister and his travail.

22. What is Hans Olsa building? What worries Hans Olsa when he sees Per Hansa? Write a theme on what you think lies behind Hans Olsa and Per Hansa's friendship.

23. What are Beret's feelings after the visit from the minister? What does Beret overhear Hans Olsa say to Per Hansa, and Per Hansa's answer? Write a theme on why you think Beret came out of her psychotic state.

24. What did the solitude do to many of the early settlers? What did many do to console themselves? What were the things the settlers feared most? Write a theme on the most fearful things the settlers had to face.

25. When did the snow start falling? What is it that Tonseten loses? Write a theme on your impression of this winter.

26. Where does Hans Olsa keep his cattle? What happens to Hans Olsa? Who does Per Hansa suggest they send for to look at Hans Olsa? Write a theme on your impression of how others regard Hans Olsa's sickness.

27. What is Beret's cardinal worry about Hans Olsa? What takes Beret away from her vigil over the sick man? Write a theme on the different attitude taken by Beret and Per Hansa toward Hans Olsa.

28. What had made Per Hansa happier during the summer and fall? What had they argued about later? What does Beret want Per Hansa to do about Hans Olsa? Write a theme on their differing points of view.

29. What does Per Hansa do to work off his anger? Who comes to Per Hansa to ask him to fetch the minister? Write a theme on why you think Per Hansa becomes so furious.

30. When his temper leaves him, where does Per Hansa go? What is Beret's final reaction when Per Hansa leaves? Write a theme on why Per Hansa took his last, impossible journey.

SELECTED BIBLIOGRAPHY

Beck, Richard. "Rölvaag, Interpreter of Immigrant Life," *North Dakota Quarterly*, XXIV, 1956.

Boynton, Percy H. "O. E. Rölvaag and the Conquest of the Pioneer," *English Journal*, 18.535-42, September, 1929.

Colcord, Lincoln. "Rölvaag The Fisherman Shook His Fist At Fate," *The American Magazine*, 105. 36-7, March, 1928.

Commager, Henry. "The Literature of The Pioneer West," *Minnesota History*, 8.319-28, December, 1927.

Jorgensen, Theodore, and Nora O. Solum. *Ole Edvart Rölvaag, a biography,* New York: Harper, 1939.

Olson, Julius E. "Rölvaag's Novels of Norwegian Pioneer Life In Dakotas," *Scandinavian Studies and Notes,* IX, 1926.

Parrington, Vernon. "Editor's Introduction," *Giants In The Earth,* New York: Harper's Modern Classics, 1929.

White, George Leroy. "O. E. Rölvaag—Prophet of the People," *Scandinavian Themes in American Fiction,* Philadelphia, 1937.

NOTES

NOTES

NOTES

NOTES

A DOLL'S HOUSE
and
HEDDA GABLER

NOTES

including
- *Introduction*
- *Biography of Ibsen*
- *Brief Summaries of Five Plays by Ibsen*
- *Act Summaries and Commentaries*
- *Critical Comments*
- *Character Analyses*
- *Selected Bibliography*
- *Selected Questions*

by
Marianne Sturman

Cliffs Notes
INCORPORATED
LINCOLN, NEBRASKA 68501

Editor	Consulting Editor
Gary Carey, M.A.	*James L. Roberts, Ph.D.*
University of Colorado	*Department of English*
	University of Nebraska

ISBN 0-8220-0614-6
© Copyright 1965
by
C. K. Hillegass
All Rights Reserved
Printed in U.S.A.

1990 Printing

Cliffs Notes, Inc.   Lincoln, Nebraska

CONTENTS

INTRODUCTION... 5
  BRIEF BIOGRAPHY OF IBSEN.............................. 5

FIVE PLAYS BY IBSEN: A BRIEF
SUMMARY... 11

A DOLL'S HOUSE
  Act I...14
  Act II..19
  Act III...23

GENERAL ANALYSIS OF A DOLL'S HOUSE
  Dramatic Structure 28
  Characters...29
  Theme 31

HEDDA GABLER
  Act I..32
  Act II...37
  Act III..40
  Act IV..42

GENERAL ANALYSIS OF HEDDA GABLER
  Introduction...45
  Characterization of Secondary Characters................45
  Characterization of Hedda Gabler 47
  Conclusion 50

DRAMA OF IBSEN.. 50

IBSEN'S CONTRIBUTIONS TO THE THEATER 52

COMPLETE LIST OF IBSEN'S DRAMAS.................. 53

SELECTED BIBLIOGRAPHY..................................... 54

SAMPLE EXAMINATION QUESTIONS...................... 54

INTRODUCTION

Once the subject of public controversy, defended only by the *avant-garde* theater critics of the nineteenth century, Ibsen's prose dramas now appear as successful television plays and are an essential part of the repertory theaters all over the world. No longer inflaming audience reactions, the dramas are now acceptable fare to the most conservative theatergoer.

Because Ibsenite drama has become part of the history of the theater, a study of his work gives us a special insight into contemporary writings. The modern "theater of the absurd," for instance, expressing a personal alienation from society, is merely another form of the social criticism which Ibsen first inspired.

With this in mind, these synopses of Ibsen's *A Doll's House* and *Hedda Gabler* and their accompanying critical commentaries are designed to help the student rediscover the significance of Ibsen's work and to guide him in evaluating the contemporary appeal—if any—of his drama.

The purpose of these Notes is to amplify the student's understanding of the plays; by no means can this booklet substitute the esthetic and emotional satisfaction to be gained from reading the plays themselves. Because Ibsen's dramas lend themselves to a variety of interpretations, the student should feel encouraged to develop his own critical approach to Ibsen from reading this volume. Designed to encourage discussion between the student and the critic represented in this writing, the Notes should be merely used as a basis for a critical dialogue. The plays themselves must supply the intellectual stimulation.

A BRIEF BIOGRAPHY OF IBSEN

Henrick Ibsen's ancestors were sea captains and businessmen, while his father was a well-to-do merchant, dealing chiefly in lumber. Ibsen was born in 1828 in Skien, a town in the south of Norway. Three brothers and a sister were born after him, but Henrick was the only member of his family to show promise. When he was eight years old, his father's business failed and the family retired to a country house. Ibsen bitterly recalled how their friends, eager to dine and drink as guests of the affluent merchant, forsook all connections with the Ibsens when they lost their financial standing.

Although the young Ibsen showed talent as a painter, his family was too poor to allow him to study art; neither could they afford to train him for his chosen profession in medicine. When he was fifteen, his father sent him to Grimstad, a small provincial town south of Skien. Here he became an apothecary's apprentice, the next best thing to medicine. In the first three years of his Grimstad life, Ibsen lived entirely alone. Too uncommunicative to make friends and too poor to seek entertainments, he read voraciously, particularly in contemporary poetry and in theology. Eventually he was the center of a small circle of young men, and during this time began to write poetry.

Learning Latin in order to prepare for the university, Ibsen studied Cicero and became deeply interested in the character of Catiline, the agitator and revolutionary who was eventually assassinated. His first play, a historical drama in verse, was an attempt to explain this elusive character. *Catiline*, however, when published at the private expense of one enthusiastic friend, received no public notice and few copies were sold.

After six dark years in the hostile atmosphere of this provincial Norwegian village, Ibsen, by extreme economy and privation, had saved enough money to leave for the capital, Christiania (Oslo). Hoping to study at the university, he enrolled in a "student factory," a popular name given to an irregular school which coached students for the entrance examinations. Here Ibsen first met his lifelong rival and contemporary, Björnstjerne Björnson, who was to be known in the future, along with Ibsen, as a national poet of Norway. Found deficient in two subjects, Ibsen failed to enter the university. At this time as well, *Catiline* was rejected by the Christiania theater, but his *The Warrior's Barrow* was accepted and performed three times in 1850.

At this period of Ibsen's youth, Norway experienced a nationalist awakening. The new literary generation, after four hundred years of Danish rule (1397-1818), sought to revive the glories of Norwegian history and medieval literature. The middle ages were glorified as well because the romantic movement was in full swing throughout Europe. Thus, when Ole Bull, the great violinist, founded a Norse theater at Bergen, the project met with enthusiastic approval from all the youthful idealists eager to subvert the influence of Danish culture.

At a benefit performance to raise money for the new venture, Ibsen presented the prologue—a poem glorifying Norway's past— which moved Ole Bull to appoint him theater poet and stage manager of the Bergen theater. This position launched Ibsen on his dramatic career. Staging more than 150 plays, including works by Shakespeare and the French dramatist Scribe, Ibsen gained as much practical experience in stagecraft as that possessed by Shakespeare and Molière. In addition to his managerial position, the poet was obliged to produce one original play a year. Although his *The Warrior's Barrow* and *St. John's Night* met with failure, the critics approved of *Lady Inger of Östraat* (1855) and *The Feast at Solhaug* (1856). In this same year, the twenty-eight year old Ibsen became engaged to Susannah Thoresen, a girl of strong personality and independent judgment, and the marriage took place two years later.

Encouraged by the success of Ole Bull's Norse theater in Bergen, enthusiasts of nationalist poetry in the capital also founded a new theater in direct competition with the conservative, Danish-influenced Christiania Theater. Asked to direct this new venture, Ibsen's promised salary was twice the amount he received at Bergen, about six hundred specie dollars.

Returning to the capital with a new play, *The Vikings at Helgeland,* Ibsen first submitted the manuscript to the old Christiania Theater where he would be free to collect royalties. At first the Danish director accepted the piece, but returned it a few months later with a flimsy excuse. This gratuitous insult sparked a hot controversy between Ibsen, Björnson, and their followers on the one hand, and the adherents of the Danish influence on the other. After five years of public controversy, the conservative director was forced to resign, while *The Vikings* became one of the chief pieces performed under the theater's new management.

Throughout these early years, the relationship between Ibsen and Björnson was very friendly. Björnson became godfather when the Ibsens' son, Sigurd, was born in 1859; when the dramatist was in serious financial straits, Björnson made every effort to raise money for him. The two men also shared the same circle of friends at this time, although Ibsen was disappointed to find that his poetic ideals were misunderstood by his gregarious contemporaries. In a poem, *On the Heights,* he expressed the view that a man who wishes to devote himself to the arts must sacrifice the usual pleasures of life; a poet must view life apart in order to find in it models for his work.

Ibsen suffered great depression during this part of his life. The varied responsibilities of his job allowed him no chance for his own creative work. In addition, the theater was doing so badly that his salary was severely reduced. Besides neglecting his work, he published no play from 1857 until *Love's Comedy* in 1862. This new anti-romantic satire received hostile reviews although it shows a maturing talent and the bold viewpoint which characterizes his later works. When the theater finally declared bankruptcy, Ibsen's despair was complete. Like Captain Alving, he became a victim of that "second-rate town which had no joys to offer—only dissipations," and spent much time in barrooms. Björnson, meanwhile, was a successful and already famous poet to whom the government awarded an annual grant of four hundred dollars to devote himself exclusively to poetic works. However Ibsen's fortunes changed in the following year when *The Pretenders,* a play glorifying the Norse heroes of the past, won an enthusiastic reception from both audience and reviewers. As a result of this success, the government awarded Ibsen a travelling scholarship to bring him in contact with the cultural trends in the rest of Europe.

Visiting Rome, Ibsen viewed for the first time the great art masterpieces of the classical and renaissance periods. In the warm, sunny climate of Italy, Ibsen felt intoxicated with his freedom from the stultifying atmosphere of Norwegian provincialism. Retiring with his family to a little town in the hills, Ibsen wrote with an inspired pen. Affected by the events of the Prusso-Danish war over Schleswig-Holstein, his interests turning from the esthetic to the ethical, Ibsen produced the colossal *Brand*.

Considered "the most stirring event in Norway's literary history of the nineteenth century," this drama won nationwide fame for its composer. The protagonist of the play, a mystical clergyman, is a courageous idealist of noble stature whose lack of love or humanity destroys his own wife and child in an uncompromising commitment to his ethical principles.

Published in the following year, *Peer Gynt* established Ibsen's international fame. This exuberant, fantasy-filled drama is the antithesis of *Brand*. The spoiled darling of a weak mother and rich father, Peer lives according to the principle of "to thyself — enough." Rather than overcoming obstacles, he goes "roundabout" and avoids facing problems. Unlike Brand, Peer never commits himself to principles unless they are to his personal benefit. The play is full of symbolic allusions and rich lyrical poetry. In 1867, the king decorated Ibsen for his achievement.

After four years in Italy, Ibsen settled down to his lifework, first in Dresden and then in Munich. His biography from this point on is more or less uneventful. Producing a new play every two years, Ibsen's dramatic powers increased and his social criticism ripened. Along with Björnson, he was considered Norway's greatest poet, but he maintained primacy as a dramatist. Honors heaped upon him and with a prosperous income, Ibsen appeared as a frock-coated and respectable middle class individual.

Almost entirely self-inspired, Ibsen was a rare genius who required no outside influence for his work. Unlike Björnson who lectured, made frequent public appearances and wrote novels and plays as well as poems, Ibsen kept to himself as much as possible. Constantly working and reworking his dramas throughout each two year period, rarely divulging, even to his family, the nature of his current writing, he single-mindedly pursued his art. Just as he gave up painting in his youth for writing poetry and drama, he now stopped composing poems, eventually relinquishing even the verse form of his earlier plays for the prose of the later works.

Harsh self-analysis was one of his life principles. In each play he expresses this constant introspection, always underscoring a thesis based on self-seeking. In *Emperor and Galilean,* for example, Julian fails to establish the "first empire" of pagan sensuality, then casts aside the "second empire" of Christian self-abnegation. As the hero expires, he envisions a "third empire," where, in the words of the biographer Zucker, "men were to find God not on Mount Olympus nor on Calvary but in their own souls, wills, and senses." Ibsen himself once wrote in a poem, that "to live is to fight with trolls in heart and brain. To be a poet is to pronounce a final judgment upon oneself."

The Norwegian commentator Francis Bull (1887–1974) sums up Ibsen's personal search:

> More deeply than ordinary men, Ibsen was split in two—a great genius and a shy and timid little philistine. In daily life he quite often did not come up to his own heroic ideals and revolutionary theories, but listened to the troll voices of narrow-minded egotism and compromise—and then, afterwards, the genius in him arose, a judge without mercy. This ever-recurring fight meant to him lifelong suffering; but it was this drama constantly going on in his own soul that made him a great dramatist and compelled him again and again to undertake a penetrating self-analysis.

Ibsen died in 1906. His tombstone, inscribed only with a hammer, the miner's symbol, alludes to a poem Ibsen wrote as a youth. Ending with "Break me the way, you heavy hammer,/To the deepest bottom of my heart," the verse is a succinct statement of the intensity of Ibsen's personal vision and of his dramatic art.

FIVE PLAYS BY IBSEN: A BRIEF SUMMARY

Ibsen's most famous plays include *A Doll's House, Ghosts, An Enemy of the People, The Wild Duck,* and *Hedda Gabler.* For the analysis of the plays not included in this volume, see the companion volume on Ibsen in "Cliff's Notes."

A DOLL'S HOUSE

Norma Helmer once secretly borrowed a large sum of money so that her husband could recuperate from a serious illness. She never told him of this loan and has been secretly paying it back in small installments by saving from her household allowance. Her husband, Torvald, thinks her careless and childlike, and often calls her his doll. When he is appointed bank director, his first act is to relieve a man who was once disgraced for having forged his signature on a document. This man, Nils Krogstad, is the person from whom Nora has borrowed her money. It is then revealed that she forged her father's signature in order to get the money. Krogstad threatens to reveal Nora's crime and thus disgrace her and her husband unless Nora can convince her husband not to fire him. Nora tries to influence her husband, but he thinks of Nora as a simple child who cannot understand the value of money or business. Thus, when Helmer discovers that Nora has forged her father's name, he is ready to disclaim his wife even though she had done it for him. Later when all is solved, Nora sees that her husband is not worth her love and she leaves him.

HEDDA GABLER

Hedda, the famous daughter of General Gabler, married George Tesman out of desperation. But she found life with him to be dull and tedious. During their wedding trip, her husband spent most of his time in libraries doing research in history for a book that is soon to be published. He is hoping to receive a position in the university.

An old friend of Hedda's comes to visit her and tells her of Eilert Lovborg, an old friend of both women. Eilert Lovborg has also written a book on history that is highly respected. In the past, however, he has lived a life of degeneration. Now he has quit drinking and has devoted himself to serious work. His new book has all the imagination and spirit that is missing in George Tesman's book. Hedda's friend, Thea Elvsted, tells how she has helped Eilert stop drinking and begin constructive work.

Later at a visit, Lovborg is offered a drink. He refuses and Hedda, jealous over the influence that Thea has on Lovborg, tempts him into taking a drink. He then goes to a party where he loses his manuscript. When George Tesman returns home with Lovborg's manuscript, Hedda burns it because she is jealous of it. Later, Lovborg comes to her and confesses how he has failed in his life. Hedda talks him into committing suicide by shooting himself in the temple. Lovborg does commit suicide later but it is through a wound in the stomach. George then begins to reconstruct Lovborg's manuscript with the help of notes provided by Thea Elvsted. Suddenly, Hedda leaves the room, takes her pistols and commits suicide.

GHOSTS

Mrs. Alving is building an orphanage as a memorial to her husband. This edifice is to be dedicated the next day, and her old friend Parson Manders has come to perform the ceremonies. In a private conversation, Mrs. Alving tells the Parson that her husband had been a complete degenerate, and she is using the rest of his money to build the orphanage so that she can leave *only* her money to her son Oswald, who has just arrived home from years and years abroad.

In a private talk with his mother, Oswald confesses that he has an incurable disease which the doctors think was inherited. Oswald, however, believes his father to have been a perfect man. Mrs. Alving, then, must confess that Mr. Alving had indeed been a degenerated man and that Oswald caught the disease from his father. Oswald knows that he is dying and wants to take the maid as his mistress so that the maid, Regina, will give him poison when he is next struck by the disease. Mrs. Alving then explains that Regina is in reality his half sister. This does not bother Oswald, but Regina refuses to stay. Oswald then tells his mother that she must administer the medicine when the next attack comes. As the play closes, Oswald begins to have his attack and his mother does not know whether to administer the poison or to endure the agony.

AN ENEMY OF THE PEOPLE

Dr. Stockmann has discovered that the new baths built in his town are infected with a deadly disease and instructs the town to repair or close the baths. The mayor, who is Dr. Stockmann's brother, does not believe the report and refuses to close the baths because it will cause the financial ruin of the town.

Dr. Stockmann tries to take his case to the people, but the mayor intercedes and explains to the people how much it will cost to repair the baths. He explains that the doctor is always filled with wild, fanciful ideas. In a public meeting, he has his brother declared an enemy of the people. The doctor decides to leave the town, but at the last minute comes to the realization that he must stay and fight for the things he believes to be right.

THE WILD DUCK

Gregers Werle has avoided his father, whom he detests, by spending fifteen years in the family mining concern. Gregers is so unattractive in appearance that he has given up all hope of marrying and having a family; instead, he has become an idealist and goes about advocating and preaching a theme of truth and purity. He calls his mission the "claim of the ideal."

His father, Old Werle, has allegedly driven his sick wife to her death by carrying on love affairs in his own home. He had once had his serving girl, Gina, as his mistress. Arranging her marriage with Hialmar Ekdal, the son of his former partner, Werle also sets the couple up in the profession of photography. Hialmar is pleased with his marriage and believes that Gina's child is his own daughter. At present, Old Werle lives with his housekeeper and between them there are no secrets.

Lieutenant Ekdal, Werle's former partner, is now a broken old man. He does odd jobs for Werle. Earlier, the company had appropriated a large quantity of lumber from a government-owned farm. Werle placed all the blame on Ekdal who was sentenced to prison. He is now living with Hialmar and Gina.

Gregers Werle comes to Hialmar and explains the claim of the ideal and tries to make Hialmar see that his marriage is based on a lie. But rather than making Hialmar happy by understanding the true nature of his marriage, Gregers only succeeds in turning Hialmar against his daughter, Hedvig. The daughter, in order to prove her love for her father who is rejecting her, takes a pistol and kills herself. Hialmar then becomes bitterly remorseful about his behavior.

A DOLL'S HOUSE

ACT I

Summary

Very cheerful, the pretty and girlish Nora Helmer enters from the outdoors, humming a tune while she deposits her parcels on the hall table. "Is that my little lark twittering out there?" calls her husband from the study, and he emerges to greet her. They talk about their improved income because Torvald has just been appointed as bank manager, and Nora chatters about Christmas presents she has just purchased for the children. Helmer suspects that his "Miss Sweet Tooth" has been "breaking rules" by indulging herself in prohibited confection. Nora denies the accusation, but the audience has seen her pop macaroons in her mouth as she came in. Deftly, Nora changes the subject and talks about decorating the tree.

The maid tells Torvald that their family friend, Dr. Rank, awaits him in his room. When Helmer has gone, another visitor arrives to see Nora, and the two women, who have not seen each other for the past ten years, are alone onstage. Christine Linde, having just returned to her home town, tells Nora all about her unfortunate life. Married unlovingly, widowed for the past three years, Mrs. Linde experienced the hardships of a woman who was forced to make her own way. She points out that her toilsome life has aged her, while

Nora is as innocent and childlike as ever. Nora declares that she too has worked and sacrificed all these years. Her toil has saved someone she loves, she boasts, and she tells Christine how she borrowed 250 pounds when Torvald's health was in such danger that he needed to go to a southern climate to improve his condition. She describes how she secretly repaid installments of the debt by stinting on her personal expenses and taking in copying work to do at night. Mrs. Linde is amazed that Nora has not mentioned the matter to her husband in all these years. He would never consent to borrowing money, Nora explains, and involuntarily she exposes the real reason for the deception: to save face for Helmer.

> How painful and humiliating it would be for Torvald, with his manly independence, to know that he owed me anything [says Nora]. It would upset our mutual relations altogether; our beautiful happy home would no longer be what it is now.

Mrs. Linde, still amazed, asks if Nora will ever reveal her secret to Helmer. Some day she shall, answers the girl with a half-smile. It may be good to "have something in reserve" in future years when she is no longer as attractive as now, "when my dancing and dressing-up and reciting have palled on him," Nora says.

The maid announces another visitor for Torvald. The newcomer, Nils Krogstad, is a lawyer and moneylender who now works at the bank. Nora seems relieved when he says he has come merely to talk with Helmer about "dry business matters." Leaving the study to allow Krogstad a private talk with his chief, Dr. Rank emerges to greet the ladies. Obsessed with thoughts of illness, the physician characterizes Krogstad as "morally diseased." Like many of his physically diseased patients, he continues, the lawyer refuses to submit to his fate, despite great agony, in the hopes of a change in his position.

This idea draws a parallel between Krogstad's situation and that of Dr. Rank. The lawyer feels his job is threatened now that Helmer is his chief, while Rank, ill with a congenital disease, is close to losing his life. With this in mind, Ibsen indicates that Krogstad clings to his respectability, or moral health, just as Dr. Rank clings to whatever physical life he has left.

Now that he has dismissed his visitor, Torvald emerges from the study and meets Mrs. Linde for the first time. Recommending that Helmer find a job for Christine, Nora makes up a little story to push her point. Her friend rushed to town, the wife relates, just as soon as she heard of Helmer's promotion in hopes of finding a place at the bank. "She is frightfully anxious to work under some clever man so as to perfect herself," concludes Nora despite Mrs. Linde's remonstrances. "Very sensible," approves Torvald, and with a well-favored "we'll see what we can do" he resumes his visit with Rank in the study. Now that Mrs. Linde has left to seek lodgings, Nora admits the nurse and loudly greets her three children.

During the noisy romp, Nora crawls under the table to play hide and seek. She emerges growling and the children shriek with laughter. No one has heard Krogstad's knock on the door. He enters, and when Nora emerges from under the table again, she gives a stifled cry at discovering her villain. Ushering the children out of the room, Nora is alone with Krogstad.

He has come, he says, to ask her to intercede with Helmer on his behalf for only her influence can protect the job which Christine Linde might take from him. He tells her that, for the sake of his growing sons, he has been working to restore his fallen position in society and he is prepared to fight for this small post in the bank as if he were "fighting for his life." Nora shows little interest until he says he is able to compel her to comply with his request. Krogstad reveals that he can prove she borrowed the 250 pounds from him by forging her father's signature. Her situation was desperate when she needed the money, Nora explains. Her father, who died soon afterward, was too ill at the time to be consulted about such matters. Surely it is no crime for a woman to do everything possible to save her husband's life, Nora declares. Forgery is a criminal act, Krogstad reminds her, and the law cares nothing about motivation. He tells her that the one false step in his own life, the one that ruined his reputation and his career "was nothing more nor nothing worse than what you have done." This is Nora's first confrontation with the harsh inflexibility of lawful society. For the last time, Krogstad asks Nora to help him keep his post. If necessary, he says, he would produce the forged bond in court. His parting words frighten Nora and she tries to distract herself by considering her Christmas decorations.

Interrupting her thoughts, Torvald comes to ask what Krogstad wanted. He is angry at Nora's evasive answer, but she finally admits that the lawyer begged her to say a good word in his behalf. Torvald becomes agreeable after Nora coaxes him to be her supervisor in choosing her costume for the fancy dress party they are to attend the next evening. Then she slowly leads the talk back to Krogstad. He once committed a forgery, Helmer tells her. "Out of necessity?" asks Nora, and he nods. Any man is allowed one false move, Torvald continues, so long as he openly confesses and accepts his punishment. But Krogstad, by his cunning, avoided the consequences of his guilt.

Just think [says Helmer] how a guilty man like that has to lie and play the hypocrite with everyone, how he has to wear a mask in the presence of those near and dear to him, even before his own wife and children. And about the children, that is the most terrible part.

He goes on to describe how "infection and poison" pollutes the very atmosphere breathed in such a home. While Nora becomes increasingly agitated, Torvald continues his lecture. In his career as a lawyer, her husband affirms, he has discovered that everyone who has "gone bad early in life" had a deceitful mother, since it is she whose influence dictates the children's moral character. He leaves Nora, stunned with horror at his words. When the nurse enters with the children she refuses to see them. "No, no, no! Don't let them come in to me," Nora pleads. It can't possibly be true, she says to herself, "Deprave my little children? Poison my home?" She is pale with terror at her thoughts while the curtain descends.

Commentary

By the end of this first act, Nora is emerging from the protection of her married life to confront the conditions of the outside world. Although she has been content in being a protected and cared-for housewife during the past eight years, and has once averted a crisis by finding a way to borrow money for the sake of Torvald's health, Nora has never learned to overtly challenge her environment.

Mrs. Linde, on the other hand, has independently faced life's challenge, although she too sought protection by marrying for the sake of financial convenience. Her harsh experience as a widow who was forced to earn her own livelihood stands in sharp contrast to the insulated and frivolous life which Nora leads. Having learned, through suffering, the value of truthful human relationships, Christine is the first person to recognize that Nora's marriage is based on deception.

The device Ibsen uses to describe the Helmer's deceptive marital relationship is the problem of Nora's debt. To prevent Torvald from discovering her secret, he shows how Nora has developed the manner of an evasive, charming adolescent whose whims and caprices her grown-up husband must indulge. This bolsters Torvald's self-image as a protector of the weak, the head of a dependent household, and the instructor of the mentally inferior.

The audience is immediately aware of Torvald's shallowness as he utters his first condescending words to his wife. Nora herself provides further evidence: when she says that Helmer might one day tire of her "reciting and dressing-up and dancing" she unknowingly describes the decadence of her marital relationship. Pedantic and pompous, Torvald sometimes seems like a father who enjoys the innocence of a favorite daughter. Setting up rules of behavior (prohibiting Nora's macaroons, for instance), instructing his wife even in her very dress, Helmer shows that he regards her as a plaything or a pet rather than an independent person. These attitudes suggest the baldly sexual nature of Helmer's marriage; the theme is later expanded in following acts until Nora recognizes her position and finds her role repulsive as well as humiliating.

Krogstad shows Nora another deceptive quality about the nature of the world: an individual is responsible for his own acts. Society punishes its lawbreaker; the innocent wife acting to save the life of her loved one is equally as guilty as the unscrupulous opportunist who acts out of expediency. Once recognizing the parallel between the "morally diseased" Krogstad and herself, Nora begins to confront the realities of the world and with this new knowledge she must draw the inevitable conclusions.

ACT II

Summary

It is later in the same day. Nora has avoided her children, fearing to pollute them. In a conversation with her old nurse, she tells the servant that the children will have to get used to seeing less of their mother from now on. This is Nora's first suggestion of withdrawing from the life she has lived up until now.

While Nora unpacks her costume from the box—the Italian fisher girl dress which reminds Torvald of their Italian honeymoon trip—Mrs. Linde enters and busies herself in sewing a tear in the garment. They discuss Dr. Rank and Christine is shocked by Nora's knowledge of inherited disease, a subject usually shielded from innocent ears. Being herself far from naive, she reproaches Nora for having borrowed the money from Dr. Rank to pay for Helmer's rest cure in Italy. Emphatically the girl denies it, for, she says, she would never allow herself placed in such a "horribly painful position" toward their old friend.

Helmer's appearance interrupts the conversation. Nora goes to greet him, and then, very prettily, coaxes her husband once more to allow Krogstad to keep his position in the bank. Nora says she is afraid he might write malicious slander about Torvald in the newspapers, threatening his new position just as her father had once been threatened. This is the part of their dialogue which illuminates the character and circumstances of Nora's father who was once a government official. Sent by the department to investigate the truth of the newspaper charges against her father, Helmer cleared his name; as a conquering hero he then married the grateful daughter.

Helmer admits that Krogstad's moral failings can be overlooked, but he is most annoyed at the moneylender's embarrassingly familiar manner toward him when there are other people around. Because they were once intimate friends, Krogstad presumes familiarity and by this attitude, Torvald says, "he would make my position in the bank intolerable." Nora is surprised, and insults Helmer by remarking how unlike him it is to take such "a narrowminded way of looking at things." He is so peeved at her estimation that he calls the maid to immediately post the letter of Krogstad's dismissal.

"Call her back, Torvald, Do you hear me, call her back," Nora pleads in panic. Taking her in his arms, he says he is not afraid of a "starving quilldriver's vengeance." Whatever happens, Helmer declares, "you may be sure that I am man enough to take everything upon myself." Nora reads much more meaning into this. "You will never have to do that," she vows. Alone onstage, Nora desperately thinks of some way to pay off the last part of the debt and free herself from Krogstad.

At this point, Dr. Rank arrives. He has come, he says, to tell her that he has one more month left to live. When the final "horrors of dissolution" begin, he will send her a card marked with a black cross for he intends to remain alone like a sick animal when it is time to die. A victim of tuberculosis of the spine, Rank denounces the "inexorable retribution" that innocent children must pay for their parent's excesses, and Nora covers her ears to prevent hearing the references to her own life and her own children.

To avoid the serious talk, Nora chatters about her dress, flirtatiously showing Rank her silk stockings. The doctor becomes serious again, expressing sorrow at being unable to leave her a token of gratitude for the friendship he enjoyed in this house. Nora, about to ask him to lend her money as a "big proof of friendship," never makes her request, for Rank responds to her hint with a passionate declaration of love. Nora rises, and quietly calls the servant to bring them more light.

As their conversation continues in the brightened room, she lapses into her former friendliness. Rank points out that she seems even more relaxed in his company than with Helmer. Nora explains that "there are some people one loves best and others whom one would almost always rather have as companions." When living with Papa, she used to steal into the maids' rooms because "they never moralized at all and talked to each other about such interesting things." She concludes with unconscious significance that "being with Torvald is a little like being with Papa."

At this point, the maid hands her Krogstad's visiting card. Finding some pretext, Nora excuses herself from Dr. Rank and confronts the moneylender who has just received Torvald's letter of dismissal. Krogstad informs Nora that he has no further interest in the money and he will keep the bond in a gesture of blackmail. With this weapon he will have the power to make Helmer guarantee his employment at the bank and to eventually attain a higher position.

Nora declares that her husband would never submit to such humiliation and hints she would rather sacrifice her life than have Torvald suffer blame for her crime. She is sure his protective nature would make him assume all the guilt, but Krogstad has a much lower opinion of Torvald's character. Turning to go, he tells her that he is leaving a letter informing Helmer of the forgery. Nora listens breathlessly as the footsteps pass downstairs. As they pause, she hears something drop into the letterbox; then the steps gradually diminish.

Returning to Christine, Nora tells of the forgery and the letter. She begs her friend to act as a witness "if anything should happen to me." Were someone to take all the blame, all the responsibility Christine must "remember that I alone did the whole thing." With mounting emotion, Nora says, "A wonderful thing is going to happen. But it is so terrible, Christine, it mustn't happen, not for all the world." Mrs. Linde insists upon paying Krogstad a visit right away. On the strength of their past love, she will ask him to recall the letter.

Torvald is accustomed at this hour to read his mail, and Nora tries to distract him. She tells him that she is so nervous about dancing the tarantella for the party that he must help her practice until the last minute. Agreeing to do nothing but instruct her dancing—not even open his mail—Torvald watches as Nora begins her dance, Rank playing the piano accompaniment. Despite her husband's instructions, Nora moves more and more violently, dancing "as if her life depended on it." Helmer suddenly cries "Stop! This is sheer madness. You have forgotten everything I've taught you." He embraces his nervous wife, suspecting that she is afraid of a letter Krogstad may have written. He promises not to look in the letterbox. "The child shall have her way," murmurs the comforting amorous husband. "But tomorrow night after you have danced — " "Then you will be free," she answers significantly.

Christine returns and tells Nora that Krogstad is out of town, but she left a letter for him. Alone, Nora resigns herself to suicide, reckoning that, until the end of the party, she has thirty-one hours left to live. "Where's my little skylark?" calls Helmer returning from the dining room to fetch her. As Nora stretches her arms out to him, the curtain falls.

Commentary

In this act, Nora learns that she alone must face the consequences of her guilt. Refusing to allow Torvald to take the blame, she prepares to kill herself.

The theme of death in this scene suggests a parallel between Nora and Dr. Rank, for the knowledge of his death coincides with her decision to commit suicide. Her tarantella is then a symbolic death dance which Rank, fittingly, plays for her on the piano. At the same time, since Helmer has chosen her dance costume to be that of a Capri fisher girl, the tarantella symbolizes their wedding, for Nora and Torvald learned the dance while honeymooning in Italy. Her dancing will be her final mortal performance, for Nora views the end of the party not only as the termination of her marriage, but as the last moments of her life.

The scene between Nora and Dr. Rank is a significant one. Not only does it underscore the "pollution and infection" which a guilty parent can pass on to his children — Nora being the guilt-ridden parent, Rank the victim of veneral disease — but it shows the youthful innocence of Nora. Accustomed to approaching her husband in a mood of adolescent flirtatiousness, Nora treats Dr. Rank the same way, as she shows him her leg dressed in the new silk stockings. When Rank responds with a declaration of love instead of amused paternity, Nora recognizes for the first time the underlying sexual nature of her relationship with Torvald. This sudden understanding prevents her asking Dr. Rank for the "big proof of friendship" which she would have been able to accept innocently from a family friend. Knowing that receiving payment from a lover places one in a "horribly painful position" reminds Nora how she has always cajoled Helmer to give her little presents of money. With this understanding, she begins to recognize how Torvald, regarding her as a romantic object, violates her personal independence.

Nora learns more about Torvald's weakness of character in this act, although she does not realize the full significance of this insight until the following scene. When Helmer tells her that he wishes to get rid of Krogstad, not because he judges him morally incompetent, but because he is ashamed to admit friendship with a man held to be disreputable, Nora observes that Torvald is quite different from the moralizing and respectable husband she has admired for eight years. Despite this insight, she still believes, as she tells Christine, that the "wonderful thing" will still take place — the proud terrible moment when Torvald discovers the forgery and takes all the guilt upon himself.

ACT III

Summary

Krogstad and Mrs. Linde are alone onstage, for the Helmers and Dr. Rank are upstairs at the masquerade party. Bitterly Krogstad reproaches Christine for renouncing their betrothal, years ago, sacrificing him in order to marry a man better able to support her and her family. After wrecking his hopes the first time, she appears again to stand in his way by taking over his hard-won position at the bank. Christine denies the charge. She says she returned to town to seek him and renew their love. Krogstad, deeply moved, is grateful for her love and faith. He says he will ask Helmer to return his letter, but Christine has changed her mind. Helmer must find out the truth, she says; all this concealment and falsehood must be exposed in order for Nora and Torvald to realize a true marriage.

After Krogstad has gone, Helmer enters, drawing Nora into the room while she struggles and protests that she wants to remain at the party a little longer. He is annoyed to find Mrs. Linde waiting up for them, and while he fetches candles, Christine tells Nora of her talk with Krogstad and counsels that "you must tell your husband all about it." With quiet resolve Nora answers, "Now I know what I must do."

Helmer is relieved when Christine finally leaves them alone. Flushed with champagne and romantic desires, he tells Nora that all this night "I have longed for nothing but you." Unable to endure his desire after watching her dance, he dragged her home. Nora twists out of his embrace. Before he can be angry, Dr. Rank enters to wish them good night, and Nora quickly senses the real reason for his visit. Turning to go, Rank says good-bye with unmistakable finality. "Sleep well," says Nora gently, adding, to his surprise, "Wish me the same."

To Nora's dismay, Torvald now goes to the letterbox. Dr. Rank has left them a visiting card marked with black; "as if he were announcing his own death," murmurs Helmer. After Nora tells him of Rank's condition, he clasps her tightly. Now that their closest friend is gone, he says, they must hold on to each other even more closely. "Do you know, Nora [Torvald whispers] I have often wished that you might be threatened by some great danger, so that I might risk my life's blood and everything for your sake."

She firmly disengages herself. "Now you must read your letters, Torvald," Nora declares. In deference to their friend's death, Torvald agrees to retire to his own room. Alone, Nora prepares to rush out to meet her own death "in the icy depths." Ready to leave her house, she gains the hall when Helmer meets her at the door of his room brandishing the letter. "You shan't save me, Torvald," cries Nora, struggling from him. In a paroxysm of self-pity and indignation, Helmer struts and shouts, vulgarly abusing his wife for bringing this shame upon him, for putting him into Krogstad's power. People might even suspect that he was responsible for the whole thing, that he prompted Nora to do the deed. At all costs the matter must be hushed up, Krogstad must be pacified. He renounces Nora as his wife. Although for the sake of appearance, she may still live in the house, she will not be allowed to raise the children and shall share no intimacy with her husband. Nora's answers are quieter and colder as Helmer talks.

Suddenly a maid, half-dressed, brings Nora a letter. Torvald grabs it, tears it open. A moment later he shouts with joy, "I am saved, Nora! I am saved," and he tears the enclosed bond into small pieces. Exultantly he forgives his wife, repeating all the platitudes he has always uttered about the cozy home he has with his skylark. "Here I will protect you like a hunted dove that I have saved from a hawk's claws," and he goes on to say, that by freely forgiving and accepting her once more as his own he has recreated his wife, giving her a new life.

By this time Nora has changed her party dress and appears in everyday clothes. "Sit down, Torvald," she says, "You and I have much to say to each other." Helmer shows surprise. "Nora, this cold set face — what is this?" Confronting her husband across a table, Nora proceeds to the "settling of accounts." First of all, she says, this is the first time in eight years "that we two, you and I, husband and wife, have had a serious conversation...We have never sat down in earnest together to try and get at the bottom of things." Over Torvald's sputtered objections she outlines the life she has been living in the "doll's house."

First she lived with her father who treated her as a toy, whose opinions and tastes she followed because he would be displeased with any disagreement, any sign of independence. "He played with me just as I used to play with my dolls. And when I came to live with you I was simply transferred from Papa's hands to yours." Torvald made all the arrangements in their life, she goes on to say, and so she never developed her own tastes or her own ideas.

When I look back on it, it seems to me as if I have been living here like a poor woman — just from hand to mouth. I have existed merely to perform tricks for you, Torvald. But you would have it so. You and Papa have committed a great sin against me. It is your fault I have made nothing of my life.

Helmer is forced to admit of some truth—though "strained and exaggerated"—in what she says. It shall be different in the future, he vows, "playtime shall be over and lesson time shall begin." She answers that he is not the man to educate her into being a proper wife. Neither is she ready to bring up her children, Nora continues, for there is another task she must first undertake. "I must try and educate myself," she says, "and I must do that for myself." That is why she is leaving him now. Finding her husband a stranger, Nora chooses to seek lodging with Christine rather than spend another night with him. Torvald points out that she has no right to neglect her most sacred duties—duties to her husband and children.

NORA: I have other duties just as sacred. Duties to myself.

HELMER: Before all else you are a wife and mother.

NORA: I don't believe that any longer, I believe that before all else I am a reasonable human being just as you are—or, at all events, that I must try and become one. I know quiet well, Torvald, that most people would think you right and that views of that kind are to be found in books; but I can no longer content myself with what most people say or with what is found in books. I must think over things for myself and get to understand them.

Torvald accuses her of loving him no longer. She nods, explaining that tonight "when the wonderful thing did not happen, then I saw you were not the man I had thought you." For such a long time she suffered with the guilty secret of her borrowed money, feeling certain that eventually the "wonderful thing" would happen. The chance came with Krogstad's letter, for Nora never imagined Torvald could submit to that man's conditions. She expected him to say proudly, "publish the thing to the whole world," and come forward to take the guilt upon himself. This expected sacrifice was the "wonderful thing" she had awaited, and to prevent it, she planned suicide.

Helmer says he is willing to toil for her day and night, bear any suffering, "but no man would sacrifice his honor for the one he loves." "It is a thing hundreds of thousands of women have always done," Nora quietly points out. She tells him that after his fear was over—"not the fear for what threatened me, but for what might happen to you"—and she became once more his little skylark, his doll, whose fragility demanded "doubly gentle care" in the future, she then realized that for eight years "I had been living with a strange man and had borne him three children." She cannot bear to think of this humiliation, Nora says, and will leave him without accepting money to live on and without communicating.

Torvald begs her to say when they can live together again. Nora sighs. "Ah, Torvald, the most wonderful thing of all would have to happen," she answers. They must both be so changed that "our life together would be a real wedlock." She turns to go, leaving Helmer, face in hands, repeating her name. Then he rises as a hope flashes across his mind. "The most wonderful thing of all—?" he murmurs. There is a noise of a door slamming shut.

Commentary

Clearly explaining the reasons for her sudden departure, Nora summarizes the entire play during her last speeches with Helmer. Discovering that her husband confuses appearance with values, that he is more concerned with his position in society than with the emotional needs of his wife, Nora is forced to confront her personal worthlessness. Rather than remain part of a marriage based on an intolerable lie, she chooses to leave her home and discover for herself the individuality which life with Helmer has denied her.

Central to this act, and in fact to the whole play, is Nora's concept of the "wonderful thing," the moment when she and Torvald would achieve a "real wedlock." In the course of the drama, she has learned that the ideal union takes place when husband and wife regard each other as rational individuals who are aware of society's demands and can fulfill their separate responsibilities with sophistication and mutual respect.

In another sense, the "wonderful thing" is merely a code word for a relationship whose values are freed from the mystique which society has attached to marriage with concept like "duty," "respectability," "cozy home," "happy family," and the rest of the stereotyped images such phrases suggest. A "real wedlock" can only be attained when a couple, deeply committed to respect each other's personal worth, work naturally and thoughtfully to fulfill ideals which their separate individualities require. Helmer, by striving for goals which have been thrust upon him in the course of an education based on social morality and verbal commitment to goals empty of feeling or commitment, deprives Nora of her sense of identity. To discover the essence of personal truth is then, the "wonderful thing" which Nora Helmer, unable to find in her marriage, must seek through her own resources.

GENERAL ANALYSIS OF *A DOLL'S HOUSE*

DRAMATIC STRUCTURE

Notable for their lack of action, Ibsen's dramas are classical in their staticism. Before the curtain rises, all the significant events have already occurred in the lives of Ibsen's characters, and it is the business of the play to reap the consequences of these past circumstances. The tight logical construction of each drama is the most important factor for the play's plausibility. With this in mind, Ibsen shows how every action of each character is the result of carefully detailed experiences in the earlier life of the person, whether in childhood, education, or genetic environment.

The author shows, for instance, that Nora's impetuosity and carelessness with money are qualities inherited from her father. Krogstad suddenly turns respectable because he needs to pass on a good name for the sake of his maturing sons. Mrs. Linde returns to town in order to renew her relationship with Krogstad. Finally, to account for Nora's secrecy with regard to the borrowed money, Ibsen shows how Torvald's way of life is devoted to maintaining appearances at the expense of inner truth.

CHARACTERS

To construct each drama even more tightly, Ibsen provides complex relationships among all his characters so that their weaknesses and strengths are reinforced by comparisons with others. Even a minor character, such as the old nurse, is significant, for she used to be Nora's nurse after the death of the girl's mother. The nurse, moreover, functions to assure the audience that Nora's children will be well-cared for in her absence, just as Nora herself was raised when her mother died. By bringing up this point early in the play, the dramatist forewarns the audience of Nora's suicide or her leaving home.

Christine Linde, Nora Helmer's contemporary, serves as a direct comparison with Ibsen's heroine. By recounting how she denied her rights to love and self-determination, by marrying for financial security, Mrs. Linde foreshadows how Nora will confront a bitter future after learning that her marriage is based on deception. Nora, according to Mrs. Linde's example, must eventually conclude, through her own sufferings, that the only way of life which can survive crises is one based on truthful relationships. The ability for Christine to rebuild her life with Krogstad can be accepted as a note of hope in Nora's case. Perhaps in the years to come, Nora and Torvald will also be able to restore their marriage.

Dr. Rank's function in the play also refers to a past occasion in Nora's life. Just as she used to seek the conversation of the maids as a refreshing change from the moralizing of her father, Nora finds amusement in Rank's companionship as a change from the tiresome cant of Torvald.

Rank's illness also serves as the physical counterpart of the moral illness of Krogstad, and by extension, of Helmer. An innocent victim of a social disease, the physician is as deeply concerned as Torvald in maintaining an exterior of well-being. Rather than allow anyone to witness the degrading aspects of his "final dissolution," Rank bids farewell to his friends and prepares to die in private. Torvald, by the same token, wishes to maintain appearances "at any cost" when he discover's Nora's disease of which he is the victim.

Torvald is shallow enough to be a mere foil for the character of Nora. Unfortunately, he is depicted with enough detail to appear a very plausible type of man, typical of many contemporary heads-of-the-family. He is a well-constructed social product, a proud specimen of a middle class husband. Because Nora has been so sheltered all her life, Torvald represents all the outside world she knows. Not only does he stand for the world of men and the world of business which has no place in her house-bound life, but he represents society at large, including all the community and legal ethics which do not concern her and religious ethics in which she has had no training. Ironically Ibsen sets up Torvald according to the same representation. For the author, Helmer stands for all the individual-denying social ills against which Ibsen has dedicated all his writing.

As a victim of his narrow view of society, Torvald inspires sympathy rather than reproach. When a man mistakes appearances for values, the basic blame must be attributed to his social environment. Ibsen, however, drives home the loathsome qualities of such a character by attributing to him a personal decadence. Implying that Torvald considers Nora merely an ornamented sex object, the author shows how he maintains amorous fantasies toward his wife: he dresses her as a Capri fisher girl and encourages her to dance in order to arouse his desires. As Helmer reinforces her girlish and immature ways, Ibsen implies an incest relationship, for Nora is made to observe that she was merely transferred from her father's tutelage to that of her husband without any change in her emotional life. It is with this final touch of perversion that Ibsen makes the character of Torvald thoroughly reprehensible to the audience.

Nora is by far the most interesting character in the play. Many critics have pointed out that such an immature, ignorant creature could never have attained the understanding and revolutionary qualities that Nora has at the time she leaves her home. Ibsen, however, has carefully constructed Nora so that her independence and far-sightedness have always shown through her adolescent capriciousness. Although her father and husband have seriously injured her practical education, Nora has retained enough native wisdom to confront an emergency. That she bungles the situation by a careless forgery provides further credence to her independence of thought as well as to her lack of sophistication. This mixture of wisdom and childishness is Nora's strongest quality. It enables her to oppose the knowledge of books and the doctrines of her worldly husband and to test by experience the social hypothesis which declares that duties to the family are the most sacred. Only an innocent creature can brave the perils of the outside world to find her identity.

Shocked audiences who objected to Nora's solution of her marital impasse and critics who considered her character unable to withstand the severe trial neglected to take account of the artistic truthfulness of the slammed door and its aftermath. One of the most common themes enduring in folklore and in less spontaneous works of art is this notion of the innocent journeying through the world to discover basic human values. The significance of these mythic themes is that only an innocent, fearless creature has the power of vision to see through the false values of sophisticated society. In Bunyan's *Pilgrim's Progress,* the story of Siegfried, Fielding's *Tom Jones,* and even in Thomas Mann's *The Magic Mountain,* we find the recurrent idea of youthful inquiry prevailing over worldly experience. Ibsen's Nora, though deriving from a much closer and realistic setting, is raised to a mythic level as she too accepts her inevitable quest, the sacred pursuit of her identity.

THEME

The interwoven themes of *A Doll's House* recur throughout most of Ibsen's works. The specific problem of this drama deals with the difficulty of maintaining an individual personality — in this case a feminine personality — within the confines of a stereotyped social role. The problem is personified as Nora, the doll, strives to become a self-motivated human being in a woman-denying man's world.

Refusing to be considered a feminist, Ibsen nevertheless expressed his view of a double-standard society. As he once forced a female character in an earlier play, *The Pillars of Society* to cry out, "Your society is a society of bachelor-souls!" he seems to have personified this male-oriented viewpoint by creating Torvald Helmer. In his notes for *A Doll's House,* Ibsen writes that the background of his projected drama "is an exclusively masculine society with laws written by men and with prosecutors and judges who regard feminine conduct from a masculine point of view." Since a woman is allegedly motivated out of love for her husband and children, it is unthinkable to her that laws can forbid acts inspired by affection, let alone punish their infraction. The outcome of this tension is that "the wife in the play is finally at her wit's end as to what is right and wrong"; she therefore loses her foothold in society and must flee the man who cannot dissociate himself from the laws of society. She can no longer live with a husband who cannot accomplish the "wonderful thing," a bridge of the mental gap which would bring his understanding and sympathies into agreement with her point of view.

It is quite impossible, however, to write a whole play with such a specific problem in mind. As characters and situations are formed by the dramatist's imagination, a more general, abstract thesis develops, with the specific problem becoming only a part of the whole. Thus *A Doll's House* questions the entire fabric of marital relationships, investigates the development of self-awareness in character, and eventually indicts all the false values of contemporary society which denies the worth of individual personality.

HEDDA GABLER

ACT I

Summary
After a six-months wedding trip, the bride and groom have returned home. Aunt Julia, Tesman's aunt, arrives to welcome them the following morning. As the curtain rises, the motherly old lady enters the well-furnished living room. She hands a bouquet of flowers to Bertha, the servant, who places them among the others which decorate the room at every corner. The aunt and the maid converse about the newlyweds, remarking with wonder and pride that the orphan nephew Miss Tesman raised is now a professor married to General Gabler's Daughter.

At this point George enters, greeting his aunt with warmth and affection. She inquires about the honeymoon, expecting to hear details of the romantic journey the young couple took touring southern Europe. Instead, Tesman delightedly recalls his tours through the archives and the collections of various libraries in order to gather research materials for his intended book, "The Domestic Industries of Brabant during the Middle Ages." His aunt, still curious, asks if George has "anything special" to tell her, if he has "any expectations," but Tesman merely answers that he expects to be appointed a professor. Aunt Julia mentions George's former colleague Eilert Lövborg. Despite publishing a recent book, she says, Lövborg has fallen a victim to his own misguided excesses. She is glad that her nephew's abilities will no longer be eclipsed by Lövborg's.

This brilliant but undisciplined young man was in love with Hedda some years ago, and they were close comrades. Confessing to her all his extravagant dissipations, his ambitions, the young man exposed his soul to this sheltered girl who was fascinated by a knowledge of life forbidden to her. When the friendship became serious, Hedda threatened Lövborg with her pistol, and he disappeared from her life from that moment on. George has no knowledge of his wife's former relationship with his friend.

The brief mention of Lövborg prefaces Hedda Gabler's entrance. She is tall and lovely, about twenty-eight years old, and responds coldly to the warmth of Miss Tesman's greeting. She is obviously bored by George's relatives, and shows no interest when her husband exclaims with pleasure over the pair of his old slippers Aunt Julia has brought him. Embroidered by Rina, the invalid sister of Miss Tesman, the slippers recall for George cherished memories of his childhood.

Hedda abruptly changes the subject, complaining that the servant has thrown her old bonnet on one of the chairs. The hat, however, belongs to Aunt Julia who has just purchased it in honor of George's bride. To overcome the embarrassment, Tesman hastily admires the bonnet, then bids his aunt admire Hedda's splendid appearance and to note how she has filled out from the journey. Angry, Hedda insists she looks the same as always, but Miss Tesman is enraptured at the implied pregnancy. Emotionally, she blesses Hedda Tesman "for George's sake." Promising to call each day, she takes her leave.

The maid announces an unexpected caller, a younger schoolmate of Hedda and a former acquaintance of George. Nervous and shy, Thea Elvsted explains the purpose of her visit. For the past year, Eilert Lövborg has lived in her house as tutor to her husband's children. The writer's conduct this past year has been irreproachable, Thea says, and he has managed to complete his successful new book while at the Elvsted's without once succumbing to temptation. Now that Lövborg has left their village, she is worried, for he has already remained a week "in this terrible town" without sending news of his whereabouts. Thea begs the Tesmans to receive him kindly if Eilert should visit them. Eager to extend hospitality to his former friend, George goes to write a letter of invitation.

Left alone with Thea, Hedda aggressively questions the reluctant younger woman, promising that they shall be close friends and address one another as "du." Thea admits that her marriage is not a happy one. She has nothing in common with her elderly husband who married her because it is cheaper to keep a wife rather than a housekeeper to look after the children.

Gaining confidence, Thea tells Hedda how a great friendship grew between Lövborg and herself until she gained an influence over him. "He never wrote anything without my assistance," she proudly declares; sharing Lövborg's work was the happiest time she has known all her life. The relationship means so much to her, that Thea has run away from home in order to live where Eilert Lövborg lives.

Yet her happiness is insecure, she tells Hedda. Although Lövborg had mentioned it only once, a woman's shadow stands between them. Hedda intently leans forward, eager to hear more. All that Lövborg said, Thea replies, is that this woman threatened to shoot him with a pistol when they parted. Mrs. Elvsted has heard about a red-haired singer whom Eilert used to visit, and she is especially worried now that this woman is in town again.

The maid announces Judge Brack, a family friend who has arranged George's affairs so that he could borrow money for his wedding trip and the villa that Hedda had set her heart on. A handsome mustached gentleman, carefully groomed and youthfully dressed, enters. About forty-five years old, Brack is very smooth in manner and bows gracefully when he and Thea are introduced.

The judge talks with Tesman about his debts while Hedda sees her guest to the door. When she returns, Brack announces his bad news: because Lövborg's book has been received so well, the writer might favorably compete for Tesman's promised professorship. George is thunderstruck, but Hedda shrugs indifferently. "There will be a sort of sporting interest in that," she says, and her husband apologizes for being unable to provide the necessities she expected: a liveried footman, a saddle horse, means for "going out into society." After Brack leaves, Hedda concludes wearily, "I shall have one thing at least to kill time with in the meanwhile—my pistols, George." She crosses to the next room, smiling coldly at her startled husband. "General Gabler's pistols!" she adds mockingly, and the curtain rings down.

Commentary

This first act, besides introducing characters, acquaints the audience with Hedda Gabler's surroundings in her new life as Mrs. Tesman. Brought up as a general's daughter accustomed to travel in aristocratic social circles, Hedda must confront her future as a housewife in a middle class household. The fact that she is pregnant reinforces her potential role as homemaker. The nature of her doom is underscored by the character of Miss Juliana Tesman who represents the older generation of domestic womanhood who has devoted her life to the care of others.

George Tesman, good natured and sentimental, assumes that the duty of a husband is merely to satisfy the domestic requirements of his wife so that she can be happy in the confines of her home. With this in mind, he agrees that they shall keep an open house—in

Hedda's chosen home—and maintain the luxuries important to proper entertaining. Believing that a woman naturally falls into household routines once she is married, George has no further insight into Hedda's temperament. Tesman's research into the "domestic industries of medieval Brabant" is an ironic symbol of his conservative, simple-minded views of married life, as well as a symbol that indicates his inability to encompass other than material details.

As to his heroine, Ibsen establishes her main symptoms of disaffection with life: a profound emotional coldness, an incapacity to interest herself in anything besides social pleasures, and a destructive desire to control the lives of others. Hedda cannot respond to the warmth of Aunt Julia, she cannot abide the idea of expecting a child, and was totally bored during her six-month wedding trip.

To further express her emotional sterility, Ibsen shows how Hedda is unable to reciprocate in a relationship. Like a young child, she can only receive without knowing how to give in return. Without reciprocating she accepts George's love and support; by pretending friendship, she learns all about Thea's personal life yet reveals no confidences of her own. Later on, when Lövborg recalls his previous relationship with Hedda, he describes how she extracted detailed confessions from him yet withheld her own self-revelations. This intense, almost morbid interest in the lives of others is another aspect of her empty emotional life. At the same time that investigating and analyzing other people's lives is one way for Hedda to gain some understanding of her own unsatisfied nature, she reveals her personal frigidity and adolescent self-centeredness.

This first act also demonstrates a pathological quality in Hedda's personality. Cruelly insulting Aunt Julia by complaining that it is the servant's bonnet lying in the chair, Hedda tries to undermine Miss Tesman's sense of worth. Compelling Thea to reveal her innermost feelings, she seems to search for Mrs. Elvsted's weaknesses so she can later use this knowledge for her own selfish purposes. Having established that his heroine is emotionally empty, yet eager to learn how other people face life's experiences, Ibsen shows how the imperious and unsubmissive Hedda tries to destroy the personal values of those whose satisfactions she cannot attain.

ACT II

Summary

As the curtain rises, Hedda is busy loading one of her pistols. There is nothing else to do besides shoot, she tells Judge Brack who has come to see Tesman. As they chat, Hedda tells him how bored she was during her wedding trip. She complains that her husband, with his everlasting talk about medieval civilization, is also boring. She is glad that Brack is a lively conversationalist who is "not at all a specialist." Her visitor wonders why Hedda accepted Tesman in the first place. "My day was done," she sighs. "I had positively danced myself tired, my dear judge." Besides, among all her suitors, George "who is correctness itself" was the one who offered marriage and a promising economic future; she saw no reason to refuse his proposal.

Brack, having himself been one of Hedda's admirers, admits that he never considered marriage. He enjoys being their family friend, he says, adding, "especially a friend of the mistress of the house." Very smoothly, he suggests that Hedda accept him as a third party in her domestic circle, for a "triangular friendship" will be convenient to all concerned. Hedda would then be able to enjoy the companionship of one who is not "a specialist" and Brack's relation with Tesman would continue as before. Hedda agrees without committing herself.

At this moment George enters. He has just visited his invalid Aunt Rina who is very sick, and he has brought some books, including the recent publication by Eilert Lövborg. Although Tesman expects to attend Brack's bachelor party this evening, he says he is eager to begin reading Lövborg's book and will come downstairs when it is time to leave. Hedda and the judge are free to continue their conversation.

Brack cannot understand why she is constantly bored; isn't she mistress of the very house she had set her heart on? She never liked this villa, replies Hedda. The matter came up when George escorted her home from a party one evening. As a pretext for conversation with the shy historian, Hedda relates, she pretended great interest in the villa they were just passing. This sham enthusiasm provided the first bond of sympathy between herself and Tesman; from this followed the courtship, engagement, and eventual marriage.

Brack observes that she requires a vocation as a relief from boredom. Hedda confesses she would like to try and push George into politics, but now that they have such meager finances this is impossible. Having the responsibility of a child would give her life an objective, Brack ventures. "No responsibilities for me," Hedda retorts angrily, and the judge remarks that her instincts are very unlike those of ordinary women. She despairs her purposeless life. "I often think there is only one thing in the world I have any turn for," Hedda observes darkly, " — boring myself to death."

Tesman, dressed for the dinner, comes to ask if Lövborg left any message. Don't expect him to join the party, Hedda says; he shall spend the evening with herself and Thea. At this moment, Lövborg enters. When they discuss his latest book, the writer denies its virtues, saying it is just a sop he threw to the critics. "This is the real book," he says drawing a packet from his coat, "the book I have put my true self into." Dealing with the "civilizing forces of the future," the manuscript excites George's curiosity and he is eager for Lövborg to read aloud from it. Tesman is further delighted when his friend promises not to compete with him for the professorship. The only interest Lövborg has in making his scheduled lecture tour, he tells George, is to accomplish a "moral victory." Refusing to drink a glass of punch with Brack and Tesman, Lövborg joins Hedda and she shows him the photograph album of their wedding journey. While she impersonally points out dull landscapes, Lövborg reminds her of the time when they were close comrades and he exposed all his secret thoughts to her. Her interest was not motivated by love, she admits, but by curiosity to learn about the outside world. "Comradeship in the thirst of life" could have continued even when they became serious lovers, Lövborg pursues. He regrets that she did not shoot him down as she threatened for he still finds her lovely and fascinating. I was afraid of a scandal, replies Hedda, and adds, "The fact that I dared not shoot you down—that was not my most arrant cowardice—that evening." Lövborg is filled with emotion. "Ah, Hedda! Hedda Gabler!" he murmurs. "Now I begin to see a hidden reason beneath our comradeship! You and I! After all, then, it was your craving for life—" and he understands that she was afraid to give herself in love.

Mrs. Elvsted appears and as they sit down together, Lövborg exclaims how courageous and lovely and inspiring Thea has been for him. When Lövborg refuses her offer of punch, Hedda subtly taunts him for feeling insecure about his temperance vow. She says that Tesman and Brack also noticed his lack of self-confidence. Again Lövborg refuses to drink, and Hedda turns smilingly to Thea. "You see," she says, "he is as firm as a rock." Thea needn't have run to her house, distracted with fear and worry about her friend's will power. Deeply injured at this lack of trust, Lövborg downs two cocktails in vengeance. Then he announces that he will, after all, join Tesman and Brack at this evening's dinner party.

Hedda assures them she will entertain Mrs. Elvsted until the writer returns to escort her home. When the men go out, Hedda comforts the agitated Thea. He will return at ten o'clock, she tells her friend. "I can see him already—flushed and fearless—with vine leaves in his hair." As the curtain falls, the victorious Hedda draws Thea, limp with exhaustion and anxiety, into the dining room for tea.

Commentary

In this act, Hedda fully expresses her desire to have power over someone. Frustrated at being unable to push her husband into a political career, incapable of maternal feelings, Hedda strives to compete with Thea for her influence over Lövborg. Having restored his liberty, she now looks forward to Eilert's fulfilling her romantic image of him as the incarnation of "the joy of life": he shall return "flushed and fearless with vine leaves in his hair!" That she has at once destroyed Thea's life work and Lövborg's morale is unimportant to Hedda; she merely wishes to have proof of her own worth by having power over someone.

At the same time that her craving for life distinguishes Hedda from "ordinary women," she shows, in this act, her deep commitment to the same bourgeois ethics which chain a woman to her domestic duties. Expressing to the judge that she accepted George Tesman because he "is correctness itself," Hedda implicitly rejects Brack's proposition of a domestic triangle: such a scandalous relationship would be repugnant to her. The judge, not recognizing that Hedda maintains such strict conventions, believes she has accepted his frank proposal.

Eilert Lövborg, however, shows more insight into Hedda's nature. When he accuses her of cowardice, he recognizes that she was too much a conformist to love an erratic and unconventional personality. Nevertheless at the time of their youthful friendship, Hedda expressed her "craving for life" by being fascinated by Eilert's intensity and brilliance; extracting detailed confessions from him was her way of vicariously experiencing a liberated and excessive way of life she was too afraid to live for herself.

ACT III

Summary

It is 7:00 the next morning. The ladies have been fitfully dozing during their nightwatch, and Hedda now sends Thea off for a good nap, promising to wake her when Lövborg arrives. When Tesman appears, Hedda is wide awake and listens eagerly as he tells her of Lövborg's extravagant behavior at the party. He was so drunk that he even dropped his manuscript without noticing, and George picked it up. Tesman praises his friend's book, admitting he feels envious for being himself unable to accomplish such brilliant work. Hedda demands the packet of papers, saying she would like to keep it awhile and read the manuscript.

At this moment George receives a telegram that his Aunt Rina is close to death. He rushes out, barely greeting Brack who has just arrived. The judge describes the rest of Eilert's activities. After the party, Lövborg landed at another soirée given by the red-haired singer, Mlle. Diana. Accusing her of robbing him, he caused such a disturbance that the police were called; to make matters worse, Lövborg resisted arrest by assaulting one of the officers.

Expecting Lövborg to seek Hedda's home as a refuge where he can meet with Mrs. Elvsted, Brack warns Hedda that he will resist any intrusion into the triangle; he wants nothing to threaten his free passage in and out of the Tesman residence. Hedda smiles mockingly at the implied threat. In other words, she calls to him as he goes, "you want to be the one cock in the basket."

When left alone, she takes the manuscript from the desk, but replaces it hastily at Lövborg's approach. Thea Elvsted emerges to greet the dishevelled writer. He has come, he sorrowfully says, to say their ways must part; from now on she must live her life without him. Thea implores him to allow her to experience her crowning satisfaction: to be with him when the book appears. There will be no book, he answers, for he destroyed the manuscript. It is as if he "killed a little child," she says in despair, and because the "child" belonged to her too, he had no right to destroy it. Thea can do nothing but return home, facing a life without any future, without any further meaning.

Alone with Hedda, Lövborg declares he is unable to try to rebuild his life. Worse than destroying the manuscript, which he had in his keeping like his own child, he just lost it during this night of "debauchery and riotness," he tells Hedda. Having so deeply failed Mrs. Elvsted, he has no future and will "only try and make an end of it all—the sooner the better." "Eilert Lövborg—listen to me," Hedda commands. She takes one of her pistols from its case and hands it to him. "Will you not try to—to do it beautifully?" she whispers. Thrusting the gun into his breast pocket, Lövborg leaves her.

Hedda, once more alone, takes the packet of papers from her desk. Sitting by the stove, she thrusts some pages into the fire. "Now I am burning your child, Thea!" she breathes. Peeling off papers, she hands them, one by one, into the flames until the entire manuscript is consumed. "Your child and Eilert Lövborg's," says Hedda with satisfaction. "I am burning—I am burning your child!"

Commentary

In this act, Hedda has confronted another frustration. Instead of seeing the awaited Lövborg rise to his full stature as a liberated artist, victoriously imbued with life's joy, she views a demoralized reveller who ruined the evening in a drunken orgy, facing, in addition, a possible jail sentence for assaulting a police officer.

Now that Thea has left the scene, however, she has one further chance of retaining her influence over Lövborg so that he will provide her with an act of "courage and freedom." Offering him the pistol, Hedda imagines that he will end his life bravely and romantically to accord with her favorite images of beauty enhanced by violence and death. Furthermore, the packet of papers she possesses represents a material hold she still has on Lövborg's destiny. By destroying the manuscript she had no share in creating or realizing, Hedda also kills the child she was unable to bear for Lövborg. By destroying that work of others which she should have accomplished herself, Hedda also destroys those constant reminders of her own inadequacies. Symbolically denying the life works of others, Hedda affirms her own unsatisfied sense of worth.

ACT IV

Summary

It is later in the evening. Miss Tesman enters, dressed in mourning. Hedda greets her, expressing regret for Rina's death. Aunt Julia plans to fill the gap in her life by finding someone to care for. Because it is necessary to live for someone, she says, she will seek an occupant for Rina's little room — some invalid in want of nursing.

After Julia leaves, George comes back, asking Hedda for the manuscript; he fears Lövborg might do himself injury before he can return it. Coolly, Hedda tells him she burned the papers. She wanted no one to put her husband "in the shade," she tells the delighted George, who never heard Hedda express her love for him.

Thea suddenly appears, apologizing for the intrusion. Having heard that Lövborg is in the hospital, she asks if they have further news of his condition. Brack, newly arrived, tells them that Lövborg wounded himself in the breast. "Not in the temple?" Hedda quickly inquires.

While Thea makes an effort to control herself, Hedda breaks the silence, declaring that there is beauty in this suicide for Eilert has made up his account with life. "He has had the courage to do the one right thing," she affirms.

Tesman expresses regret that Lövborg has left the world without bequeathing it "the book that would have immortalized his name." Mrs. Elvsted fumbles in her dress pocket. Producing many scraps of paper — "all the loose notes he used to dictate from" — she suggests that they might reconstruct the book. Tesman is delighted. Having spent his career organizing other people's manuscripts, he is eager to dedicate himself to putting together Lövborg's notes. Forgetful of everything but the papers spread on the table before them, Thea and George begin the task.

Hedda languidly reclines in the armchair, Judge Brack at her side. It gives her a new feeling of freedom, she tells her admirer, to know that a "deed of deliberate courage is still possible in this world — a deed of spontaneous beauty." Brack dispels her illusions, informing her of the true circumstances of Lövborg's death which he did not disclose to Thea. Lövborg did not die voluntarily, he tells the astonished Hedda. The police discovered the body in Mlle. Diana's boudoir, Lövborg had forced his way into the singer's apartment, talking wildly about a "lost child." While they struggled, the pistol in his breast pocket discharged itself, and he died from a bullet wound in his bowels.

Her shocked face is disfigured by an expression of loathing and despair. "Oh, what a curse is it that makes everything I touch turn ludicrous and mean?" she cries out. Brack remains unperturbed. One more disagreeable aspect remains, he says, for Lövborg must have stolen the pistol. Hedda passionately denies this, and Brack nods. He says that if someone were to identify the pistol, she herself would be drawn into the scandal. "So I am in your power, Judge Brack," says Hedda. "You have me at your beck and call from this time forward." Leaning closer, he assures her that he shall not "abuse his advantage."

Hedda stands behind Mrs. Elvsted, passing her hands affection-ately through her friend's hair. "Here you are, Thea, sitting with Tesman—just as you used to sit with Eilert Lövborg," and she asks whether she can inspire George as well as she used to inspire Eilert. Intently working, her husband exclaims that he begins to feel in-spired by Thea, and asks his wife to return to Judge Brack. "Is there nothing I can do to help you two?" asks Hedda. "No, nothing in the world," George answers without looking up.

He suggests to Thea that she rent the room in Aunt Julia's apartment; without disturbing Hedda they can meet there every evening to work on the manuscript. "But how am I to get through the evenings out here?" Hedda calls from the back room. Tesman assures her that the judge shall look in on her every now and then. Brack gaily adds that he shall visit "every blessed evening," and that "we shall get on capitally together, we two!" Loud and clear, Hedda answers, "Yes, don't you flatter yourself we will, Judge Brack. Now that you are the one cock in the basket—" A shot rings out. Tesman, Mrs. Elvsted, and Brack discover Hedda stretched lifeless on the sofa; she had shot herself in the temple.

Commentary

Going beyond the destruction that Hedda began in the previous acts, circumstances depicted in the final scene destroy the life's work of each other character. Julia's sister dies, leaving the old aunt with no one to care for; Tesman relinquishes his work on medieval Brabant; Thea has definitely lost Lövborg; and Hedda confronts profound disillusion when she learns of Eilert's ignoble death.

The secondary characters, however, all find vocational rebirth as they confront their ruined life purposes. Thea, having saved Lövborg's notes, begins, with George Tesman, to conceive a new "child"; the professor so expert at assembling other people's manu-scripts can dedicate his abilities to reconstruct his dead friend's brilliant ideas; and Julia can again care for her beloved nephew now that Hedda is gone.

Hedda alone faces a life without a future. Deprived of her satis-faction at the beauty of Eilert's suicide, she learns that she was in fact responsible for the abhorrent manner of Lövborg's death. Her ideal of freedom, courage and beauty turns into a loathsome reality. Judge Brack applies the final vulgar touch to a situation that Hedda already finds repulsive; he alone can inform the police of the facts that would implicate her in a shocking scandal. The conventional Hedda must either succumb to Brack's power or face a public inquiry. Now that even her husband has no further need of her, no one depends upon Hedda at this point. On the other hand she is unwillingly enthralled by the ruthless Brack. Deprived of freedom, Hedda faces either "boring herself to death" or committing a valiant suicide.

GENERAL ANALYSIS OF *HEDDA GABLER*

INTRODUCTION

Written in 1890, *Hedda Gabler* is a high point in Ibsen's creative life. Although the "social dramas" of his prose period depict full-bodied and believable characters, Ibsen achieved a psychological depth in *Hedda Gabler* that his later works never surpassed. Having investigated the feminine character in a male-oriented society in *Doll's House* and *Ghosts,* Ibsen enlarged his scrutiny to encompass the full pathology of the social female. Although Hedda Gabler is an example of perverted femininity, her situation illuminates what Ibsen considered to be a depraved society, intent on sacrificing to its own self-interest the freedom and individual expression of its most gifted members.

CHARACTERIZATION OF SECONDARY CHARACTERS

As usual in Ibsen's tightly constructed dramas, each character provides, by comparison, insight into every other character. The characterizations of Thea Elvsted and Miss Juliana Tesman, unlike Hedda, depict women who submit to their socially-imposed feminine roles and derive satisfaction from their lives: they devote themselves to the unselfish tasks of raising children and serving to inspire masculine creativity. Julia, for instance, has raised George Tesman who became a promising academician, and now that the nephew has grown up, she takes care of her invalid sister. Thea, after having married an unloving elderly man in order to care for his household, has found a satisfying life assisting and inspiring the work of a creative and brilliant writer. Through her devotion, Lövborg has been able to channel his undisciplined energies to produce according to his potential. His masterpiece, the product of their mutual inspiration, is the natural child which, through love, Thea and Eilert have conceived.

Compared to Aunt Julia and Mrs. Elvsted, Hedda seems an unnatural woman. Refusing to relinquish her freedom, she regards childbearing as loathsome and destroys the manuscript conceived by Thea and Lövborg as if she were murdering her own child. Degrading Aunt Julia by insulting her new bonnet, Hedda expresses hostility toward her husband as well as his relatives.

Hedda's emotional sterility is counterparted by Judge Brack's lack of compassion. Unlike Hedda, Brack has a profession and is free to amuse himself without overstepping the masculine social conventions. This parallel between them illustrates the double standards of society which denies rights of self-expression to women.

The emptiness of Brack's emotional life is underscored by his attributes of vulgarity and lechery. Willing to first compromise Hedda's respectability as a married woman, he has no compunctions about using blackmail as a weapon guaranteeing his selfish ends. Like Hedda, Brack wishes to substitute power over someone for love which he is unable to give.

Tesman's bumbling ordinariness contrasts vividly and humorously with Lövborg's flamboyant and creative brilliance. Where George writes about the "domestic industries of Brabant in the middle ages", Eilert works on a book dealing with the "civilizing forces" of humanity in the future. Tesman delights in researching among old manuscripts, while Lövborg considers the problems of the future.

Seeing only an inexperienced bride, the husband admires Hedda for her qualities of beauty and poise and expects that she will learn to love him at some future time. Hedda's former lover, on the other hand, is fascinated by her "craving for life" and has insight into her cowardly retreat to convention. Tesman is eager for his professional appointment which will guarantee his ability to support his household, while Lövborg looks forward to the "moral victory" he will achieve from delivering his scheduled lectures. Solicitous to his aunts, Tesman cherishes sentimental reminders of the love and care he received as a child (as shown by his delight at receiving an old pair of slippers Rina embroidered for him); Lövborg, recognizing that the past is irreclaimable, breaks with Thea when he loses the manuscript they have written together.

Ibsen sets the brilliant writer as an exact counterpart to the medieval scholar in many ways. Where one is erratic, the other is steady; one deals with abstract and philosophical problems, the other concerns himself with concrete and detailed minutiae. Because of these qualities, however, Lövborg, a representation of the discontinuity in living a free life, cannot carry on his work. Tesman, on the other hand, representing the continuity of living a structured life, is able to take up Lövborg's work and eventually fulfill the writer's promise of greatness. With this situation, Ibsen seems to imply a balance of human forces: the erratic genius is necessary to provide the impelling idea, but the character who is gifted with less imagination and an ability to work hard at concrete details is the one able to realize the idea.

CHARACTERIZATION OF HEDDA GABLER

Placed in similar crises as previous Ibsen heroines, Hedda Gabler faces an impasse in her life. Sharing Nora's craving for freedom, and Mrs. Alving's compliance with social conventions, Hedda finds no outlet for her personal demands; she is constantly torn between her aimless desire for freedom and her commitment to standards of social appearance. Refusing to submit to her womanly destiny, Hedda has such an unsatisfied craving for life that she is incapable of being emotionally involved with others.

When Nora Helmer recognized her own unsatisfied needs, she left her husband and children. Considering her most "sacred duty" was to find herself, she left home to discover her personal worth through facing life's experiences before being able to relate to others. Like Nora, Hedda Gabler is a stranger to herself. However, lacking Nora's daring and defiance of conventions, she is unable to undergo the trials of self-evaluation and becomes a morbidly self-vindictive, destructive virago, capable only to strike out against the successful socially conforming individuals who represent an implicit reproach to her uninformed cravings. In the play, Ibsen provides enough information to show how Hedda's problem is the product of her special background.

Raised by her military father, Hedda must have grown up in an atmosphere of strict discipline and conformity to rules. Becoming a beautiful sought-after young woman, she attended many social affairs but never found anyone to marry; probably she was not rich enough to interest the eligible bachelors of high social standing.

As a product of the nineteenth century, where women were destined to become either respectable old maids like George's aunts, or humble housekeepers like Mrs. Elvsted, Hedda is an anomaly. Instead of preparing his daughter for wifehood or mother-hood, General Gabler taught her to ride and shoot, skills symbolic of the military mystique which became for Hedda the basis of her fascination with the violent and the romantic. Inheriting from her father, whose forbidding portrait hangs in the Tesman's drawing room, his pride and coldness as well as his imperious commanding attitude toward others of a lower rank, Hedda lacks compassion for weak and submissive creatures like Thea and Aunt Julia but has a respect for power and independence, qualities she finds in Brack and Lövborg.

Since it was unthinkable at the time for a woman to receive either an intellectual or a professional education, Hedda's intelligence remained stultified. Unable to recognize the demands of her individuality, she remains enslaved to a standard of social conventionality and can only admire from afar the forbidden world where there is freedom of expression and an uninhibited exuberance of life. Eilert Lövborg provides Hedda with the vicarious experience of an individual who enjoys an unfettered creative life. She drew sustenance from his soul's outpourings as he told her of his dreams, his work, and his excessive way of life. At the same time, Hedda was too ignorant and inexperienced to accurately evaluate Lövborg's character; she regarded him not as a creature of reality, but as the person—and realization of her adolescent quest for the romantic. When Lövborg made serious demands on her, Hedda rejected him. Stultified at the emotional level of an adolescent and repelled by his unconventionality, she could no longer tolerate the intensity of an actual relationship and shrank from responding to his demands.

George Tesman, on the other hand, is an acceptable husband especially because he makes no demands on Hedda's emotional incapacity. Posing no threat to her internal security, he is able to provide her with material security and to indulge her tastes for luxury and an active social life. Besides being sincerely fond of his bride, Tesman satisfies Hedda's conventional standards (he is "correctness itself") and leaves her imagination free to indulge her demand for independence and courage.

Having thus married to innure herself from any internal threats, Hedda coldly plans to base her life on the enjoyment of external advantages. The drama begins at this point, and develops characters and events which swiftly undermine Hedda's system of values. Her pregnancy is the first disturbance to her calculated system of inner protection. Hedda then learns that Tesman's appointment may be deferred, a situation which deprives her of luxury and active social entertainments.

It is significant that Lövborg, Hedda's romantic ideal of the free and life-intoxicated hero, becomes George's professional rival. According to her conception, Eilert's free spirit must have somehow been conquered, or she must have deceived herself as to his true nature. In either case, Hedda is deprived of her favorite ideal and must try to reinstate the old Lövborg in order to maintain an equilibrium between fantasy and reality. When she discovers that Thea Elvsted has preempted her former power over Eilert, now temperate, hard-working, and successful, she overrides Thea to gain the desired influence over Lövborg. This too backfires, for his liberation from Thea's steadying influence becomes a sordid debauchery that ends with Eilert's ignoble death. Thus, all Hedda's expectations dissolve into a vulgar residue that she cannot accept.

Brack administers the final blow to her dream of independence when he threatens her with blackmail. After all her efforts at manipulating others so that she can remain free of fettering responsibilities and slavish domestic attachments, Hedda learns that she is forever at Brack's "beck and call" if she wishes to avoid being involved in a sordid scandal. With this final disillusion, Hedda no longer has a life worth facing. In a tragic attempt to "do it beautifully" she puts a bullet through her temple.

CONCLUSION

The problem of Hedda Gabler illuminates the universal problem of woman in a society built by men. Like Mrs. Alving and Nora Helmer, Hedda must make an independent decision about her life. Women, however, in all but the most progressive societies, are barred from participating in the world outside their households and are not equipped for independence outside their families. Thus, Hedda Gabler, despite a profound craving for independence, has no personal resources with which to realize self-responsibility. Having the desire, but not the ability, for a constructive effort at self determination, she becomes a modern Medea, expressing her frustration in destructive attempts at self-realization. Not having any positive influence in the world, Hedda Gabler can only define herself negatively: she destroys what she cannot accept. Undermining her husband with her coldness, denying her pregnancy, destroying Thea's life-work, burning Lövborg's creative product, ruining the child-manuscript, and finally, committing suicide, are all perverted attempts to satisfy her "craving for life." By depicting the pathology of a frustrated woman in *Hedda Gabler,* Ibsen declares his most powerful protest against the double standard society.

DRAMA OF IBSEN

Although the plays are interesting for their social message, Ibsen's dramas would not survive today were it not for his consummate skill as a technician. Each drama is carefully wrought into a tight logical construction where characters are clearly delineated and interrelated, and where events have a symbolic as well as actual significance. The symbolism in Ibsen's plays is rarely overworked. Carefully integrated to unify the setting, events, and character portrayals, the symbols are incidental and subordinate to the truth and consistency of his picture of life.

Having been interested in painting as a youth, Ibsen was always conscious of making accurate observations. As a dramatist, he considered himself a photographer as well, using his powers of observation as a lens, while his finished plays represented the proofs of a skilled darkroom technician. The realism of his plays, the credibility of his characters, the immediacy of his themes attest to these photographic skills at which Ibsen so consciously worked. Among his countless revisions for each drama, he paid special heed to the accuracy of his dialogue. Through constant rewriting, he brought out the maximum meaning in the fewest words, attempting to fit each speech into the character of the speaker. In addition, Ibsen's ability as a poet contributed a special beauty to his terse prose.

The problems of Ibsen's social dramas are consistent throughout all his works. Georg Brandes, a contemporary critic, said of Ibsen, as early as the 1860's, that "his progress from one work to the other is not due to a rich variety of themes and ideas, but on the contrary to a perpetual scrutiny of the same general questions, regarded from different points of view." In *A Doll's House*, he especially probed the problems of the social passivity assigned to women in a male-oriented society. After considering the plight of Nora Helmer, he then investigated what would happen had she remained at home. The consequence of his thoughts appear in *Ghosts*. Going one step further, Ibsen investigated the fallacies inherent in his own idealism. Much as Pastor Manders applies empty principles to actual situations, Gregers Werle is shown trying to impose an idealistic viewpoint when circumstances demand that individuals can only accept their lives by clinging to "life lies." Although *The Wild Duck* differs in treatment from *Hedda Gabler*, the plays both have protagonists who find in their imaginations an outlet for their frustrations. *Hedda Gabler*, however, with its emphasis on individual psychology, is a close scrutiny of a woman like Nora Helmer or Mrs. Alving who searches for personal meaning in a society which denies freedom of expression.

Professor Koht sums up the dramatist's investigations:

> The thing which filled [Ibsen's] mind was the individual man, and he measured the worth of a community according as it helped or hindered a man in being himself. He had an ideal standard which he placed upon the community and it was from this measuring that his social criticism proceeded.

Secondary to, and in connection with, his idea that the individual is of supreme importance, Ibsen believed that the final personal tragedy comes from a denial of love. From this viewpoint we see that Torvald is an incomplete individual because he attaches more importance to a crime against society than a sin against love. The same is true for Pastor Manders. Hedda Gabler is doomed to a dissatisfied life because she too is unable to love, and Hedvig's tragic suicide is the result of her pathetic attempt to recall her father's affections. In Ibsen's other plays, particularly *Brand*, this theme is of primary importance.

In an age where nations were striving for independence, Ibsen's sense of democracy was politically prophetic. He believed, not that "right" was the prerogative of the mass majority, but that it resided among the educated minority. In the development and enrichment of the individual, he saw the only hope of a really cultured and enlightened society.

IBSEN'S CONTRIBUTIONS TO THE THEATER

Until the latter part of the nineteenth century, theater remained a vehicle of entertainment. Insights into the human condition were merely incidental factors in the dramatist's art. Ibsen, however, contributed a new significance to drama which changed the development of modern theater. Discovering dramatic material in everyday situations was the beginning of a realism that novelists as different as Zola and Flaubert were already exploiting. When Nora quietly confronts her husband with "Sit down, Torvald, you and I have much to say to each other," drama became no longer a mere diversion, but an experience closely impinging on the lives of the playgoers themselves. With Ibsen, the stage became a pulpit, while the dramatist exhorting his audience to reassess the values of society, became the minister of a new social responsibility.

COMPLETE LIST OF IBSEN'S DRAMAS

VERSE 1850 Catiline
1850 The Vikings Barrow
1853 St. John's Night
1855 Lady Inger of Ostraat
1856 The Feast of Solhaug
1857 Olaf Liljekraus
1858 Vikings of Helgeland
1862 Love's Comedy
1864 The Pretenders
1866 Brand
1867 Peer Gynt
1869 The League of Youth (prose)
1873 Emperor and Galilean (blank verse)

PROSE 1877 Pillars of Society
1879 A Doll's House
1881 Ghosts
1882 Enemy of the People
1884 The Wild Duck
1886 Rosmersholm
1888 The Lady from the Sea
1890 Hedda Gabler
1892 The Master Builder
1894 Little Eyolf
1896 John Gabriel Borkman
1900 When We Dead Awaken

SELECTED BIBLIOGRAPHY

Brian W. Downs, *A Study of Six Plays by Ibsen;* Cambridge, England: 1950.

Edmund Gosse, *Henrik Ibsen.*

Halvdan Koht, *The Life of Ibsen,* translated by R. L. McMahon and H. A. Larsen; 2 vols.; New York: 1931.

Janko Lavrin, *Ibsen, An Approach;* London, 1950.

M. S. Moses, *Henrik Ibsen, the Man and His Plays;* Boston: 1920.

George Bernard Shaw, *The Quintessence of Ibsenism;* Ayot St. Lawrence edition, vol. 19; London: 1921.

Hermann J. Wiegand, *The Modern Ibsen,* New York: 1925.

Adolph Edouard Zucker, *Ibsen, the Master Builder;* New York: 1929.

SAMPLE EXAMINATION QUESTIONS

1. Using specific examples, discuss how Ibsen's "progress from one work to the other" is due to a "perpetual scrutiny of the same general questions regarded from different points of view."

2. Do you feel that Ibsen's drama is "dated"? To defend your view, cite dramatic themes in these plays which you consider to be universal, or limited in scope.

3. Why does Ibsen choose a woman as his protagonist in these plays?

4. At least one character in each play prefers his imaginary view of life to a realistic viewpoint. With this in mind, discuss the life-views of Torvald Helmer and Hedda Gabler.

5. In what ways do the vocations of Torvald Helmer and George Tesman provide additional insight into their character?

6. In each play, show how the first act forewarns the audience of almost all the forthcoming events in the rest of the drama.

7. Point out some instances where Ibsen is able to "externalize" inner problems by using effective symbols.

8. Devise an alternative ending for *A Doll's House* trying not to violate Ibsen's dramatic thesis. Defend either your new conclusion or the inviolability of Ibsen's original ending.

9. Explain the symbolic significance of hereditary disease in *A Doll's House*.

10. Why is *Hedda Gabler* rather than *Hedda Tesman* the title of the drama?

11. What is the symbolic value ascribed to Hedda's pistol.

12. Why is it dramatically necessary for Hedda Gabler to burn Lövborg's manuscript?

NOTES

GHOSTS,
AN ENEMY
OF THE PEOPLE,
THE WILD DUCK

NOTES

including
- *Introduction and Biography*
- *Brief Summaries*
- *Act-by-Act Summaries and Commentaries*
- *Critical Notes and Character Analyses*
- *Questions for Discussion*
- *Selected Bibliography*

by
Marianne Sturman

INCORPORATED

LINCOLN, NEBRASKA 68501

Editor	Consulting Editor
Gary Carey, M.A.	*James L. Roberts, Ph.D.*
University of Colorado	*Department of English*
	University of Nebraska

ISBN 0-8220-0617-0
© Copyright 1965
by
C. K. Hillegass
All Rights Reserved
Printed in U.S.A.

1989 Printing

Cliffs Notes, Inc.   Lincoln, Nebraska

CONTENTS

Topic   Page

INTRODUCTION... 5

A BRIEF BIOGRAPHY OF IBSEN.. 5

FIVE PLAYS BY IBSEN: A BRIEF SUMMARY...................... 11

GHOSTS

    Act I.. 14

    Act II... 19

    Act III.. 23

GENERAL ANALYSIS

    Theme.. 27

    Structure and Technique.. 28

    Character Analysis.. 29

    Symbolism.. 31

AN ENEMY OF THE PEOPLE

    Act I.. 32

    Act II... 35

    Act III.. 39

    Act IV.. 42

    Act V... 44

GENERAL ANALYSIS.. 46

    Structure and Technique.. 46

    Character Analysis.. 47

THE WILD DUCK

    Introduction.. 50

    Act I.. 50

    Act II... 52

    Act III.. 56

    Act IV.. 58

    Act V... 60

GENERAL ANALYSIS

    Structure, Technique, and Theme................................. 65

    Characters and Symbols... 66

    Character Analysis.. 68

DRAMA OF IBSEN.. 69

IBSEN'S CONTRIBUTIONS TO THE THEATER..................... 71

COMPLETE LIST OF IBSEN'S DRAMAS............................. 71

SELECTED BIBLIOGRAPHY... 72

QUESTIONS FOR DISCUSSION.. 73

INTRODUCTION

Once the subject of public controversy, defended only by the *avant-garde* theater critics of the nineteenth century, Ibsen's prose dramas now appear as successful television plays and are an essential part of the repertory theaters all over the world. No longer inflaming audience reactions, the dramas are now acceptable fare to the most conservative theatergoer.

Because Ibsenite drama has become part of the history of the theater, a study of his work gives us a special insight into contemporary writings. The modern "theater of the absurd," for instance, expressing a personal alienation from society, is merely another form of the social criticism which Ibsen first inspired.

With this in mind, these synopses of Ibsen's *The Wild Duck, Ghosts,* and *An Enemy of the People* and their accompanying critical commentaries are designed to help the student rediscover the significance of Ibsen's work and to guide him in evaluating the contemporary appeal — if any — of his drama.

The purpose of these Notes is to amplify the student's understanding of the plays; by no means can this booklet substitute the esthetic and emotional satisfaction to be gained from reading the plays themselves. Because Ibsen's dramas lend themselves to a variety of interpretations, the student should feel encouraged to develop his own critical approach to Ibsen from reading this volume. Designed to encourage discussion between the student and the critic represented in this writing, the Notes should be merely used as a basis for a critical dialogue. The plays themselves must supply the intellectual stimulation.

A BRIEF BIOGRAPHY OF IBSEN

Henrik Ibsen's ancestors were sea captains and businessmen, while his father was a well-to-do merchant, dealing chiefly in lumber. Ibsen was born in 1828 in Skien, a town in the south of Norway. Three brothers and a sister were born after him, but Henrik was the only member of his family to show any promise. When he was eight years old, his father's business failed and the family retired to a country house. Ibsen bitterly recalled how their friends, eager to dine and drink as guests of the affluent merchant, forsook all connections with the Ibsens when they lost their financial standing.

Although the young Ibsen showed talent as a painter, his family was too poor to allow him to study art; neither could they afford to train him for his chosen profession in medicine. When he was fifteen, his father sent him to Grimstad, a small provincial town south of Skien. Here he became an apothecary's apprentice, the next best thing to medicine. In the first three years of his Grimstad life, Ibsen lived entirely alone. Too uncommunicative to make friends and too poor to seek entertainments, he read voraciously, particularly in contemporary poetry and in theology. Eventually he was the center of a small circle of young men, and during this time began to write poetry.

Learning Latin in order to prepare for the university, Ibsen studied Cicero and became deeply interested in the character of Catiline, the agitator and revolutionary who was eventually assassinated. His first play, a historical drama in verse, was an attempt to explain this elusive character. *Catiline,* however, when published at the private expense of one enthusiastic friend, received no public notice and few copies were sold.

After six dark years in the hostile atmosphere of this provincial Norwegian village, Ibsen, by extreme economy and privation, had saved enough money to leave for the capital, Christiania (Oslo). Hoping to study at the university, he enrolled in a "student factory," a popular name given to an irregular school which coached students for the entrance examinations. Here Ibsen first met his lifelong rival and contemporary, Björnstjerne Björnson, who was to be known in the future, along with Ibsen, as a national poet of Norway. Found deficient in two subjects, Ibsen failed to enter the university. At this time as well, *Catiline* was rejected by the Christiania theater, but his *The Warrior's Barrow* was accepted and performed three times in 1850.

At this period of Ibsen's youth, Norway experienced a nationalist awakening. The new literary generation, after four hundred years of Danish rule (1397-1818), sought to revive the glories of Norwegian history and medieval literature. The middle ages were glorified as well because the romantic movement was in full swing throughout Europe. Thus, when Ole Bull, the great violinist, founded a Norse theater at Bergen, the project met with enthusiastic approval from all the youthful idealists eager to subvert the influence of Danish culture.

At a benefit performance to raise money for the new venture, Ibsen presented the prologue — a poem glorifying Norway's past — which moved Ole Bull to appoint him theater poet and stage manager of the Bergen theater. This position launched Ibsen on his dramatic career. Staging more than 150 plays, including works by Shakespeare and the French dramatist Scribe, Ibsen gained as much practical experience in stagecraft as that possessed by Shakespeare and Moliére. In addition to his managerial position, the poet was obliged to produce one original play a year. Although his *The Warrior's Barrow* and *St. John's Night* met with failure, the critics approved of *Lady Inger of Ostratt* (1855) and *The Feast of Solhaug* (1856). In this same year, the twenty-eight year old Ibsen became engaged to Susannah Thoresen, a girl of strong personality and independent judgment, and the marriage took place two years later.

Encouraged by the success of Ole Bull's Norse theater in Bergen, enthusiasts of nationalist poetry in the capital also founded a new theater in direct competition with the conservative, Danish-influenced Christiania theater. Asked to direct this new venture, Ibsen's promised salary was twice the amount he received at Bergen, about six hundred specie dollars.

Returning to the capital with a new play, *The Vikings at Helgeland*, Ibsen first submitted the manuscript to the old Christiania theater where he would be free to collect royalties. At first the Danish director accepted the piece; but returned it a few months later with a flimsy excuse. This gratuitous insult sparked a hot controversy between Ibsen, Björnson, and their followers on the one

8

hand, and the adherents of the Danish influence on the other. After five years of public controversy, the conservative director was forced to resign, while *The Vikings* became one of the chief pieces performed under the theater's new management.

Throughout these early years, the relationship between Ibsen and Björnson was very friendly. Björnson became godfather when the Ibsens' son, Sigurd, was born in 1859; when the dramatist was in serious financial straits, Björnson made every effort to raise money for him. The two men also shared the same circle of friends at this time, although Ibsen was disappointed to find that his poetic ideals were misunderstood by his gregarious contemporaries. In a poem, *On the Heights,* he expressed the view that a man who wishes to devote himself to the arts must sacrifice the usual pleasures of life; a poet must view life apart in order to find in it models for his work.

Ibsen suffered great depression during this part of his life. The varied responsibilities of his job allowed him no chance for his own creative work. In addition, the theater was doing so badly that his salary was severely reduced. Besides neglecting his work, he published no play from 1857 until *Love's Comedy* in 1862. This new anti-romantic satire received hostile reviews although it shows a maturing talent and the bold viewpoint which characterizes his later works. When the theater finally declared bankruptcy, Ibsen's despair was complete. Like Captain Alving, he became a victim of that "second-rate town which had no joys to offer—only dissipations," and spent much time in barrooms. Björnson, meanwhile, was a successful and already famous poet to whom the government awarded an annual grant of four hundred dollars to devote himself exclusively to poetic works. However Ibsen's fortunes changed in the following year when *The Pretenders,* a play glorifying the Norse heroes of the past, won an enthusiastic reception from both audience and reviewers. As a result of this success, the government awarded Ibsen a travelling scholarship to bring him in contact with the cultural trends in the rest of Europe.

Visiting Rome, Ibsen viewed for the first time the great art masterpieces of the classical and renaissance periods. In the warm, sunny climate of Italy, Ibsen felt intoxicated with his freedom from the stultifying atmosphere of Norwegian provincialism. Retiring with his family to a little town in the hills, Ibsen wrote with an inspired pen. Affected by the events of the Prusso-Danish war over Schleswig-Holstein, his interests turning from the esthetic to the ethical, Ibsen produced the colossal *Brand*.

Considered "the most stirring event in Norway's literary history of the nineteenth century," this drama won nationwide fame for its author. The protagonist of the play, a mystical clergyman, is a courageous idealist of noble stature whose lack of love for humanity destroys his wife and child in an uncompromising commitment to his ethical principles.

Published in the following year, *Peer Gynt* established Ibsen's international fame. This exuberant, fantasy-filled drama is the antithesis of *Brand*. The spoiled darling of a weak mother and rich father, Peer lives according to the principle of "to thyself — enough." Rather than overcoming obstacles, he goes "roundabout" and avoids facing problems. Unlike Brand, Peer never commits himself to principles unless they are to his personal benefit. The play is full of symbolic allusions and rich lyrical poetry. In 1867, the king decorated Ibsen for his achievement.

After four years in Italy, Ibsen settled down to his lifework, first in Dresden and then in Munich. His biography from this point on is more or less uneventful. Producing a new play every two years, Ibsen's dramatic powers increased and his social criticism ripened. Along with Björnson, he was considered Norway's greatest poet, but he maintained primacy as a dramatist. Honors heaped upon him and with a prosperous income, Ibsen appeared as a frock-coated and respectable middle class individual.

Almost entirely self-inspired, Ibsen was a rare genius who required no outside influence for his work. Unlike Björnson who lectured, made frequent public appearances and wrote novels and plays as well as poems, Ibsen kept to himself as much as possible. Constantly working and reworking his dramas throughout each two year period, rarely divulging, even to his family, the nature of his current writing, he single-mindedly pursued his art. Just as he gave up painting in his youth for writing poetry and drama, he now stopped composing poems, eventually relinquishing even the verse form of his earlier plays for the prose of the later works.

Harsh self-analysis was one of his life principles. In each play he expresses this constant introspection, always underscoring a thesis based on self-seeking. In *Emperor and Galilean*, for example, Julian fails to establish the "first empire" of pagan sensuality, then casts aside the "second empire" of Christian self-abnegation. As the hero expires, he envisions a "third empire," where, in the words of the biographer Zucker, "men were to find God not on Mount Olympus nor on Calvary but in their own souls, wills, and senses." Ibsen himself once wrote in a poem, that "to live is to fight with trolls in heart and brain. To be a poet is to pronounce a final judgment upon oneself."

The British commentator, Francis Bull, sums up Ibsen's personal search:

More deeply than ordinary men, Ibsen was split in two—a great genius and a shy and timid little philistine. In daily life he quite often did not come up to his own heroic ideals and revolutionary theories, but listened to the troll voices of narrow-minded egotism and compromise—and then, afterwards, the genius in him arose, a judge without mercy. This ever-recurring fight meant to him lifelong suffering; but it was this drama constantly going on in his own soul that made him a great dramatist and compelled him again and again to undertake a penetrating self-analysis.

Ibsen died in 1906. His tombstone, inscribed only with a hammer, the miner's symbol, alludes to a poem Ibsen wrote as a youth. Ending with "Break me the way, you heavy hammer,/ To the deepest bottom of my heart," the verse is a succinct statement of the intensity of Ibsen's personal vision and of his dramatic art.

FIVE PLAYS BY IBSEN: A BRIEF SUMMARY

Ibsen's most famous plays include *A Doll's House, Hedda Gabler, Ghosts, An Enemy of the People,* and *The Wild Duck.* For the analyses of the plays not included in this volume, see the companion volume on Ibsen, published by Cliffs Notes.

A DOLL'S HOUSE

Norma Helmer once secretly borrowed a large sum of money so that her husband could recuperate from a serious illness. She never told him of this loan and has been secretly paying it back in small installments by saving from her household allowance. Her husband, Torvald, thinks her careless and childlike, and often calls her his doll. When he is appointed bank director, his first act is to relieve a man who was once disgraced for having forged his signature on a document. This man, Nils Krogstad, is the person from whom Nora has borrowed her money. It is then revealed that she forged her father's signature in order to get the money. Krogstad threatens to reveal Nora's crime and thus disgrace her and her husband unless Nora can convince her husband not to fire him. Nora tries to influence her husband, but he thinks of Nora as a simple child who cannot understand the value of money or business. Thus, when Helmer discovers that Nora has forged her father's name, he is ready to disclaim his wife even though she had done it for him. Later when all is solved, Nora sees that her husband is not worth her love and she leaves him.

HEDDA GABLER

Hedda, the daughter of the famous General Gabler, married George Tesman out of desperation. But she found life with him to be dull and tedious. During their wedding trip, her husband spent most of his time in libraries doing research in history for a book that is soon to be published. He is hoping to receive a position in the university.

An old friend of Hedda's comes to visit her and tells her of Eilert Lövborg, an old friend of both women. Eilert Lövborg has also written a book on history that is highly respected. In the past, however, he has lived a life of degeneration. Now he has quit drinking and has devoted himself to serious work. His new book has all the imagination and spirit that is missing in George Tesman's book. Hedda's friend, Thea Elvsted, tells how she has helped Eilert stop drinking and begin constructive work.

Later at a visit, Lövborg is offered a drink. He refuses and Hedda, jealous over the influence that Thea has on Lövborg, tempts him into taking a drink. He then goes to a party where he loses his manuscript. When George Tesman returns home with Lövborg's manuscript, Hedda burns it because she is jealous of it. Later, Lövborg comes to her and confesses how he has failed in his life. Hedda talks him into committing suicide by shooting himself in the temple. Lövborg does commit suicide later but it is through a wound in the stomach. George then begins to reconstruct Lövborg's manuscript with the help of notes provided by Thea Elvsted. Suddenly, Hedda leaves the room, takes her pistols and commits suicide.

GHOSTS

Mrs. Alving is building an orphanage as a memorial to her husband. This edifice is to be dedicated the next day, and her old friend Parson Manders has come to perform the ceremonies. In a private conversation, Mrs. Alving tells the Parson that her husband had been a complete degenerate, and she is using the rest of his money to build the orphanage so that she can leave only *her* money to her son Oswald, who has just arrived home from years and years abroad.

In a private talk with his mother, Oswald confesses that he has an incurable disease which the doctors think was inherited. Oswald, however, believes his father to have been a perfect man. Mrs. Alving, then, must confess that Mr. Alving had indeed been a degenerated man and that Oswald caught the disease from his father. Oswald knows that he is dying and wants to take the maid as his mistress so that the maid, Regina, will give him poison when he is next struck by the disease. Mrs. Alving then explains that Regina is in reality his half sister. This does not bother Oswald, but Regina refuses to stay. Oswald then tells his mother that she must

dminister the medicine when the next attack comes. As the play
:loses, Oswald begins to have his attack and his mother does not
.now whether to administer the poison or to endure the agony.

AN ENEMY OF THE PEOPLE

Dr. Stockmann has discovered that the new baths built in his
own are infected with a deadly disease and instructs the town to
epair or close the baths. The Mayor, who is Dr. Stockmann's
orother, does not believe the report and refuses to close the baths
oecause it will cause the financial ruin of the town.

Dr. Stockmann tries to take his case to the people, but the may-
or intercedes and explains to the people how much it will cost to
epair the baths. He explains that the Doctor is always filled with
vild, fanciful ideas. In a public meeting, he has his brother declared
an enemy of the people. The doctor decides to leave the town, but
at the last minute comes to the realization that he must stay and
ight for the things he believes to be right.

THE WILD DUCK

Gregers Werle has avoided his father, whom he detests, by
spending fifteen years in the family mining concern. Gregers is so
unattractive in appearance that he has given up all hope of marry-
ng and having a family; instead, he has become an idealist and goes
about advocating and preaching a theme of truth and purity. He
:alls his mission the "claim of the ideal."

His father, Old Werle, has allegedly driven his sick wife to her
death by carrying on love affairs in his own home. He had once had
his serving girl, Gina, as his mistress. Arranging her marriage with
Hialmar Ekdal, the son of his former partner, Werle also sets the
:ouple up in the profession of photography. Hialmar is pleased with
his marriage and believes that Gina's child is his own daughter. At
present, Old Werle lives with his housekeeper and between them
there are no secrets.

Lieutenant Ekdal, Werle's former partner, is now a broken old
man. He does odd jobs for Werle. Earlier, the company had

appropriated a large quantity of lumber from a government owne
farm. Werle placed all the blame on Ekdal who was sentenced t
prison. He is now living with Hialmar and Gina.

Gregers Werle comes to Hialmar and explains the claim of the
ideal and tries to make Hialmar see that his marriage is based on
a lie. But rather than making Hialmar happy by understanding the
true nature of his marriage, Gregers only succeeds in turning Hal-
mar against his daughter, Hedvig. The daughter, in order to prove
her love for her father who is rejecting her, takes a pistol and kills
herself. Hialmar then becomes bitterly remorseful about his behavior

GHOSTS

ACT I

Summary

Regina Enstrand, a young girl in service for Mrs. Alving, appears in the garden. She tries to prevent her father, Jacob Engstrand,
from entering. The rain makes the old man even more disreputable
looking than usual, and Regina makes it clear she is ashamed of his
coarseness and vulgar appearance. Engstrand has come to ask Regina
to live with him and work for him in his planned "seamen's home."
He says he has saved enough money from doing carpentry work on
the new orphanage to begin this enterprise and now that she has
grown into "such a fine wench" she would be a valuable asset. He
clearly implies that this seamen's home will be a high class brothel.
Regina says she has her own plans for the future, especially since
Oswald Alving has just returned from his studies in Paris.

Pastor Manders enters after Engstrand has left. He talks with
Regina about her father. Since Engstrand requires a strong influence
to keep him from drinking, Manders suggests that Regina, out of
filial duty, return to live with him and be "the guiding hand" in her
father's life. Regina says she would rather seek a place in town as
a governess.

While the girl goes to fetch Mrs. Alving, Manders peruses some books on the table. He gives a start after reading the title page of one, and with increasing disapproval looks at some others. Cordially and affectionately, Mrs. Alving comes in to greet him. Politely inquiring after Oswald, Manders then asks who reads these books. Shocked to find they are hers, he wonders how such readings could contribute to her feeling of self-reliance, as she puts it, or how they can confirm her own impressions. What is objectionable about the books, she asks. "I have read quite enough about them to disapprove of them," he answers. "But your own opinion—" she pursues. He talks as if to a child:

> My dear Mrs. Alving, there are many occasions in life when one has to rely on the opinions of others. That is the way in the world, and it is quite right that it should be so. What would become of society otherwise?

He now wishes to discuss their mutual business—the Captain Alving Orphanage—built by Mrs. Alving in honor of her late husband. Although she has left all the arrangements to Manders, he wants to ask whether they should insure the buildings. To her prompt "of course," he raises objections since the orphanage is dedicated to "higher causes." He points out that his fellow clergymen and their congregations might interpret the insurance to mean "that neither you nor I had a proper reliance on Divine protection." As Mrs. Alving's advisor he himself would be the first attacked by "spiteful persons" who would publicly slander him. She assures him that under these conditions she would not wish the buildings insured.

Speaking of insurance, Mrs. Alving mentions that the building nearly caught fire yesterday from some burning shavings in the carpenter's shop. She says she has heard that Engstrand is often careless with matches. Manders makes excuses because the "poor fellow" has so many anxieties. "Heaven be thanked," he says, "I am told he is really making an effort to live a blameless life...Why he assured me so himself." Manders thinks it would be best for Engstrand if Regina returned to live with him, but Mrs. Alving's firm "No!" is definitive.

Oswald appears, bearing so much likeness to his dead father that Manders is startled; Mrs. Alving quickly insists that her son takes after her. During their conversation, Oswald shocks the pastor by depicting the fidelity and beauty of family life among the common-law marriages of his fellow painters in Paris. Disapproving of artists in the first place, Manders sputters indignantly at such circles "where open immorality is rampant." He cannot understand how "the authorities would tolerate such things" and is even more dismayed when Mrs. Alving later declares that Oswald "was right in every single word he said." In her loneliness, she continues, she has come to the same conclusions as her son, that the married men of good social standing are capable of the greatest acts of immorality.

It is his duty to speak now, but not just as a friend, Manders says, "it is your priest that stands before you just as he once did at the most critical moment of your life." He reminds her how she came to him after the first year of marriage, refusing to return to her husband. She softly reminds him that the first year was "unspeakably unhappy." To crave for happiness is simply to be "possessed by a spirit of revolt," he answers. Bound in marriage by a "sacred bond" her duty was "to cleave to the man you had chosen;" though a husband be profligate, a wife's duty is to bear the cross laid upon her shoulders by "a higher will," Manders continues. It was imprudent for her to have sought refuge with him at the time, and he is proud to have had the strength of character to lead her back "to the path of duty" and back to her husband.

Having defaulted in her wifely duty, she also neglected her duty as a mother, Manders goes on. Because she sent Oswald to boarding schools all his life rather than educating him at home, the child has become a thorough profligate. "In very truth, Mrs. Alving, you are a guilty mother!" Manders exhorts.

These conclusions are unjust, Mrs. Alving answers, for Manders knew nothing of her life from that moment on. He must know now "that my husband died just as great a profligate as he had been all his life." In fact, she tells him, a disease he contracted from his lifelong excesses caused his death. Manders gropes for a chair. To think that all the years of her wedded life were nothing but "a hidden abyss of misery" makes his brain reel. She says that her husband's scandalous conduct invaded the walls of this very house for she witnessed Alving's approaches to the servant Joanna. "My husband had his will of that girl," Mrs. Alving continues, "and that intimacy had consequences." Only later on does Manders discover that the "consequences" are Regina.

Mrs. Alving goes on to describe how she sat up with her husband during his drinking bouts, being his companion so he would not leave the house to seek others. She had to listen to his ribald talk and then, with brute force, bring him to bed. She endured all this for Oswald's sake, sending him to boarding schools when he was old enough to ask questions. As long as his father was alive, Oswald never set foot in his home.

Besides thoughts of her son, she also had her work to sustain her, Mrs. Alving tells Manders. Too besotted to be useful, her husband depended on her to keep him in touch with his work during his lucid intervals. She improved and arranged all his properties, and she is converting his share of the estate into the "Captain Alving Orphanage." By this gesture Mrs. Alving hopes to "silence all rumors and clear away all doubt" as to the truth of her husband's life. None of his father's estate shall pass on to Oswald; "my son shall have everything from me," she states.

Grumbling at "this everlasting rain," Oswald returns from his walk. When Regina announces that dinner is ready, Oswald follows her into the dining room to uncork the wines. Meanwhile Manders and Mrs. Alving discuss the dedication ceremony for the opening of the orphange tomorrow. She regards the occasion as the end of "this long dreadful comedy." After tomorrow she shall feel as if the dead husband had never lived here. Then "there will be no one else here but my boy and his mother," she declares. They hear a quiet scuffle from the next room, then Regina's whisper, "Oswald! Are you mad? Let me go!" Horror-struck, Mrs. Alving hoarsely whispers to Manders, "Ghosts. The couple in the conservatory — over again." He is bewildered. Then knowledge dawns. "What are you saying! Regina — ? Is she — ?" His hostess nods helplessly. The curtain comes down.

Commentary

As the first act functions to introduce the characters, the central problem of the play, as well as the essential story line, the playwright carefully forewarns his audience of the themes he will develop in subsequent acts. In fact, the first scene of a well written drama often presents a complete analogy of the whole play. With this in mind, the author imparts special significance to the order of appearance of his characters.

Regina is the first to appear, showing by dress and demeanor that she is a properly reared servant maid. As she talks with her father, the audience recognizes that, though she is of vulgar stock, she has aspirations to gentility. This is shown as she uses her little knowledge of French.

Engstrand's appearance keynotes the theme of a depraved parent who ensnares his child in his own dissolution, especially as the carpenter asks Regina to join him in his planned enterprise. Implying that she is not his true-born daughter, Ibsen also introduces the theme that children, although unaware of their origins, inherit qualities from their parents. As Regina accuses her father of being able to "humbug" the reverend, and later on showing how Manders accepts Engstrand's hypocrisy for fact, Ibsen introduces the idea that society recognizes phrase-mongering rather than integrity of thought and action as a standard of moral respectability.

Pastor Manders appears next; suggesting that Regina return to live with her father shows how he allies himself with Jacob Engstrand. The respectability and social orthodoxy which he expresses in phrases like "daughter's duty" rather then defining his principles through thoughtful investigations, show that Manders supports anyone whose cant agrees with his own.

After Manders peruses the books, Mrs. Alving enters. The audience senses that she is separated from the pastor by an abyss created by her intellect and experience, as symbolized by the books. Arranged on the table which stands between them, these volumes are in fact their first subject of dissension. One does not have to read them to denounce them, Manders states. He is content to accept the opinions of others. By her answers, Mrs. Alving shows she is no longer satisfied by dogma; she must learn truth through her own experience.

Since Manders indicates no ability to learn anything not expressed in pious formulas, we cannot expect his character to change during the drama. Mrs. Alving, on the other hand, welcoming controversy and opposing the results of her experience to what she has always been taught, is fully prepared to face the full impact of events forthcoming in the rest of the play. This quality marks Mrs. Alving as the protagonist of the drama. Having established these intellectual qualities of the mother, Ibsen now brings forth Oswald. As the entire product of Mrs. Alving's life, he presents the greatest problem she will confront.

This arrangement of character introduction suggests the opposing tensions of the play. Regina, her dead mother, and Engstrand parallel Oswald, his mother, and the dead Mr. Alving. One side represents that part of society whose members have loose morals, aspirations to gentility, and who grab at whatever opportunity for self-betterment they can; the other side represents the best in society, a group whose members are cultured, propertied, and have strong ethics. In the middle, as if he were a fulcrum balancing the extremes, stands Pastor Manders. Already appearing as a moralizing but empty-headed standard of society, denouncing Mrs. Alving's intellectual inquiry and supporting Engstrand's hypocrisy, the character of Manders allows the audience to foresee the thesis of the drama: that a society which unwittingly destroys individuality and encourages deceit perpetrates disease—physical as well as emotional—upon its youthful members.

ACT II

Summary

The scene is unchanged, but now it has stopped raining and a mist obscures the outside landscape. With dinner finished, Oswald out for a walk, and Regina busy with the laundry, Mrs. Alving and Manders continue their conversation. She tells how she managed to hush up the scandal of Alving's conduct by providing Joanna with a handsome dowry and having her respectably married off to Jacob Engstrand. Manders is shocked that the carpenter lied to him by confessing of his "light behavior" with Joanna and so deceived the pastor to perform the ceremony. How could a man, "for a paltry seventy pounds" allow himself to be bound in marriage "to a fallen woman." Mrs. Alving points out that she was married to a "fallen man," but Manders says the two cases are as different as night and day. Yes, his hostess agrees, there was a great difference in the price paid, "between a paltry seventy pounds and a whole fortune"; besides, her family arranged the marriage, for she was in love with someone else at the time. To answer her meaningful glance, Manders weakly concludes that at least the match was made "in complete conformity with law and order." I often think that law and order are "at the bottom of all the misery in the world," retorts Mrs. Alving. She regrets her lifelong cowardice. Were she not such a coward in the name of law and order, she says, "I would have told Oswald all I have told you, from beginning to end." Manders points out that she taught her son to idealize his father and as a mother she must feel forbidden to shatter his illusions. "And what about the truth?" asks Mrs. Alving. "What about his ideals?" responds Manders, underlining Ibsen's basic equation that "ideals" equal "lies".

Although Mrs. Alving wishes to quickly find a post for Regina before Oswald gets her in trouble, she regrets her cowardice. To prevent further deceit she should rather encourage the marriage or any other arrangement, she tells the pastor. Manders is shocked that she can suggest a relationship based on incest; as to her so-called cowardice, he denies there was any better way to tell Oswald of his father. By being a coward, Mrs. Alving explains, she succumbs to ghosts:

> I am frightened and timid because I am obsessed by the presence of ghosts that I never can get rid of...When I heard Regina and Oswald in there it was just like seeing ghosts before my eyes. I am half inclined to think we are all ghosts, Mr. Manders. It is not only what we have inherited from our fathers and mothers that exists again in us, but all sorts of old dead ideas and all kinds of old dead beliefs and things of that kind. They are not actually alive in us, but there they are dormant all the

same, and we can never be rid of them. Whenever I take up a newspaper and read it I fancy I see ghosts creeping between the lines. There must be ghosts all over the world. They must be countless as the grains of the sands, it seems to me. And we are so miserably afraid of the light, all of us.

Manders blames these strange ideas on her reading—this "subversive, free-thinking literature"—but she says her ideas come from suffering what Manders himself praised "as right and just what my whole soul revolted against as it would against something abominable." You think it was wrong for me to entreat you as a wife to return to your lawful husband "when you came to me half distracted and crying, 'Here I am, take me!' " asks the pastor. "I think it was," she answers.

Manders declares he can no longer allow a young girl to remain in her house and Regina must go home to her father's care. At this moment there is a knock at the door. Engstrand enters, respectfully requesting the reverend to lead "all of us who have worked so honestly together" on the orphanage building in some concluding prayers. Closely questioning Engstrand about his marriage and other matters, Manders offers the carpenter a chance to explain what must "lie so heavy" on his conscience. The old man makes a fine show of piousness and sensitive feelings as he tells his story. Manders, with tears in his eyes at his flawless life, offers Engstrand a strong handshake of faith and friendship. The pastor, turning to his hostess, asks if she doesn't think that we must be "exceedingly careful" before "condemning our fellow men." "What I think is that you are, and always will remain, a big baby, Mr. Manders," she answers, and thinks that "I should like to give you a big hug!" Hurriedly, the pastor goes out to conduct the prayer meeting.

Discovering Oswald in the dining room, Mrs. Alving sits down with him for a chat. Her son complains that, besides being constantly tired, the lack of sunshine prevents him from painting. This is no ordinary fatigue, he tells his mother, but it is part of a sickness a Paris doctor diagnosed for him. He was told he had this "canker of disease" since his birth. Oswald continues that "the old cynic said, 'The sins of the fathers are visited on the children'." To prove that his father lived a dutiful, virtuous life, the boy read some of his mother's letters to the doctor. As Mrs. Alving softly repeats, "The sins of the fathers!" Oswald confesses of a single instance of "imprudence" that must have infected him. He despairs that he threw his life away for a brief pleasure and asks his mother for something to drink to drown "these gnawing thoughts." Regina brings in a lamp and fetches champagne.

"I can't go on bearing this agony of mind alone," Oswald tells his mother. He would like to take Regina with him and leave home. Because she has "the joy of life in her," Regina will be his salvation. "The joy of life?" asks Mrs. Alving with a start, "Is there salvation in that?" Regina brings more wine and Oswald asks her to fetch a glass for herself. At her mistress' nod, the girl obeys and takes a seat at the table.

Mrs. Alving wants to know more about the "joy of life." People here at home are taught to consider work as a curse and punishment for sin and that life is a state of wretchedness, Oswald explains. No one believes that in Paris, where "the mere fact of being alive is thought to be a matter for exultant happiness. There is light there and sunshine and a holiday feeling," he says. Oswald says he must leave home. If not, "all these feelings that are so strong in me would degenerate into something ugly here," he tells his mother. She regards him steadily for a moment. Now, for the first time, she murmurs, "I see clearly how it all happened. And now I can speak." She is about to tell Oswald and Regina the truth when Manders suddenly enters, cheerful from having spent an "edifying time" at the prayer meeting. He says he has decided that Engstrand needs help with the sailors' home and Regina must go and live with him.

"Regina is going away with me," Oswald states, and Manders turns to Mrs. Alving in bewilderment. "That will not happen either," she declares, and despite the pastor's pleading is about to speak openly. At this moment they hear shouting outside and through the conservatory windows they see a red glare. The orphange is ablaze. "Mrs. Alving, that fire is a judgment on this house of sin!" cries Manders. As they all rush out to the orphange, he is left wringing his hands. "And no insurance," he moans, and then follows them.

Commentary

Formally developing the drama, the second act brings out details and enlarges the action, characterizations and motives which were introduced in the first act. Moreover, the acceleration of events taking place in this scene, their effects heightened by the rich symbolism in Mrs. Alving's "ghosts" speech, leads the audience to await the final nemesis or judgment that will occur in Act III. More specifically, the purpose of this second part is to focus attention on Oswald and complete the characterizations of the secondary characters. By so doing, the playwright can fully disclose the consequences when individuals live by old beliefs and traditional dogma and then assess the guilt for this crime.

Exposing the history of their previous relationship, the conversation between Mrs. Alving and Pastor Manders provides the audience with a completed portrait of the clergyman. First showing Manders' hypocrisy and self-centeredness, Ibsen sums him up as a "big baby." The dramatist, by allowing Engstrand to recite the humbug story of his virtuous life, fully depicts the moral irresponsibility of the carpenter. With these two characters completely developed, Ibsen may now investigate the problem of Mrs. Alving and dwell on the fruits of her cowardice, Regina and Oswald.

Having in common their "joy of life" inherited through their father, Regina and Oswald show their youthful innocence by being unaware of their near-incest relationship. When Mrs. Alving discovers that Oswald, like his father before him, feels that this exuberance of life will degenerate in the sanctimonious home atmosphere, she suddenly understands why her husband became a dissipated drunkard. To prevent further deceit, she prepares Oswald and Regina to comprehend the truth of their origins and the nature of their heritage. As she begins to say the words that will raze these old lies of her past life, they discover the orphanage is ablaze. The symbol of hypocrisy and deceit—a worthy institution to serve society—is destroyed in the moment of truth.

ACT III

Summary

The scene still takes place in Mrs. Alving's home, but it is night time. By now the fire is out, the entire orphanage burned to the ground. While Mrs. Alving has gone to fetch Oswald, Regina and Manders receive Engstrand. "God help us all," he says piously and clucking sympathetically says that the prayer meeting caused the fire. Whispering that "Now we've got the old fool, my girl," he tells Manders, the only one carrying a candle, that he saw the pastor snuff the light and toss the burning wick among the shavings. The distraught reverend is beside himself. The worst aspect of this matter, he says, will be the attacks and slanderous accusations of the newspapers. By this time Mrs. Alving has returned. She considers the fire merely as a business loss; as to the property and the remaining capital in the bank, Manders may use it as he likes. He thinks he may still turn the estate into "some useful community enterprise" and Engstrand is hopeful for his support of the seamen's home. Gloomily, Manders answers that he must first await the published results of the inquiry into the cause of the fire. Offering himself as "an angel of salvation," Engstrand says he will himself answer to the charge. Relieved and breathless, Manders eagerly grasps his hand. "You are one in a thousand," he declares. "You shall have assistance in the matter of your sailors' home, you may rely upon that."

United in friendship, Engstrand and Manders prepare to leave together. Announcing to Mrs. Alving that his enterprise shall be called "The Alving Home," the carpenter concludes, "And if I can carry my own ideas about it, I shall make it worthy of bearing the late Mr. Alving's name." The double entendre is unmistakable to everyone except Manders.

Oswald returns so depressed that Regina is suspicious he may be ill. Mrs. Alving now prepares to tell them both what she started to divulge in the previous scene. What Oswald told her about the joy of life suddenly sheds new light upon everything in her own life, she tells them, for his father, so full of "irrepressible energy and exuberant spirits" in his young days "gave me a holiday feeling just to look at him." Then this boy had to settle in a second-rate town which had none of the joy of life to offer him but only dissipations:

He had to come out here and live an aimless life; he had only an official post. He had no work worth devoting his whole mind to; he had nothing more than official routine to attend to. He had not one single companion capable of appreciating what the joy of life meant; nothing but idlers and tipplers—and so the inevitable happened.

What was the inevitable, asks Oswald, and his mother answers that he had himself described how he would degenerate at home. "Do you mean by that Father—?" and she nods:

Your poor father never found any outlet for the overmastering joy of life that was in him. And I brought no holiday spirit into his home either. I had been taught about duty and that sort of thing that I believed in so long here. Everything seemed to turn upon duty—my duty or his duty—and I am afraid that I made your poor father's home unbearable to him, Oswald.

Then why did she not write him the truth in her letters, demands the son, and she can only say she never regarded it as something a child should know about. "Your father was a lost man before ever you were born," says Mrs. Alving, and all these years she has kept in mind that Regina "had as good a right in this house—as my own boy had." To their bewilderment she answers quietly, "Yes, now you both know."

"So Mother was one of that sort too," Regina muses. Then she announces her desire to leave them to make good use of her youth before it is wasted. With Oswald sick, she does not wish to spend her life looking after an invalid for "I have the joy of life in me too, Mrs. Alving." From now on she shall make her home in the "Alving Home." Mother and son are alone onstage.

"Let us have a little chat," says Oswald beckoning her to sit beside him. Before he divulges the truth about his fatigue and inability to work he warns her she mustn't scream. The illness itself is hereditary, he continues, and "it lies here (touching his forehead) waiting. At any moment, it may break out." She stifles a cry. At the time he had a serious attack in Paris, Oswald goes on, the doctor told him he would never recover from another one. The disease is a lingering one—the doctor likened it to a "softening of the brain"—and it will leave him hopeless as a vegetable.

Showing his mother a dozen morphia tablets, Oswald says he needed Regina's strength and courage to administer "this last helping hand." Now that Regina is gone, however, his mother must swear that she will give him them herself when it is necessary. Mrs. Alving screams and tries to dash out for the doctor, but Oswald reaches the door first and locks it. "Have you a mother's heart and can bear to see me suffering this unspeakable terror?" he cries out. Trying to control herself, Mrs. Alving trembles violently. "Here is my hand on it," she says.

Outside day is breaking. Oswald is seated quietly in an armchair near the lamp. Cautiously bending over him, Mrs. Alving straightens up, relieved:

It has only been a dreadful fancy of yours, Oswald [she chatters]. ...But now you will get some rest, at home with your own mother, my darling boy...There now, the attack is over. You see how easily it passed off...And look, Oswald, what a lovely day we are going to have. Now you will be able to see your home properly.

She rises and puts out the lamp. In the sunrise the glaciers and peaks in the distance are bathed in bright morning light. Oswald, with his back toward the window, suddenly speaks. "Mother give me the sun." Regarding him with amazement she quavers, "What did you say?" Dully, Oswald repeats, "The sun—the sun." She screams his name. As before, he only says, "The sun—the sun." She beats her head with her hands. "I can't bear it! Never!" she screams. Then, passing her hands over his coat, she searches for the packet of pills. "Where has he got it? Here!" Then she cries, "No, no no!—Yes!—No, no!" Mrs. Alving stares at her son in speechless terror. Oswald remains motionless. "The sun—the sun," he repeats monotonously, and the curtain falls.

Commentary

As in a Greek tragedy, the protagonist's "tragic flaw" involves not only himself, but his children, in the consequences of guilt. In this act Mrs. Alving receives the full penalty for her guilt of substituting a sense of duty for the "joy of life." Her submission to ancient social standards destroys the creative mind of her artist son and similarly destroys Regina's blooming womanhood. The "ghosts" of heredity reappear as Oswald succumbs to syphilitic paresis and as Regina goes to find her future in a brothel. Mrs. Alving can only administer the final stroke — the mortal dose of morphia — to complete the destruction of Oswald she had so unwittingly begun.

With a dramatic flourish, Ibsen uses the environment as an ironic "objective correlative" to underscore the tragedy. As the dawn breaks over a spectacular mountain landscape, Oswald is thrust into the unending darkness of his lingering doom. The long awaited sunshine, so badly needed by Oswald to continue his painting, arrives only to illuminate catastrophe. By the same token, the light of truth has come too late for Mrs. Alving to avoid the consequences of her lifelong deceit.

GENERAL ANALYSIS

THEME

As if to answer the hosts of critics who denounced the "vulgar untruths" they discovered in *A Doll's House,* Ibsen developed another facet of the same idea when he published *Ghosts* two years later. According to Halvdan Koht, one of his biographers, "Mrs. Alving is in reality nothing but a Nora who has tried life and her inherited teachings and who has now taken a stand." Having sacrificed love for conformity, Mrs. Alving must face the tragic consequences of denying her personal needs.

In essence, the problems Ibsen probes in *A Doll's House* are the same as those of *Ghosts:* the relation between past and future, and the relationship between the race and community on one hand, and the individual on the other. Society perpetuates itself by handing down from one generation to another a set of beliefs and customs so that new individuals can take part in the culture and contribute to its perpetuation. Ibsen, however, shows how these principles may degenerate until they actually destroy the very individuals that the social system is created to protect and nurture. He insists that these "ghosts" of old beliefs and outdated piety must be reexamined in the light of each individual's experience; if not, the most gifted of society's children will face destruction.

Having himself suffered all his life under the conservatism of Norwegian provincialism, Ibsen personally found how such a society destroys the "joy of life" in its creative intellects leaving bitterness and frustration.

STRUCTURE AND TECHNIQUE

As in most of Ibsen's problem plays, *Ghosts* begins at the collective climax in the lives of its characters. The play deals only with the consequences of these past lives and does not need to take place in more than one twenty-four hour vigil. Although the relationships among the characters are close and lifelong, only the crowding of emotions and events within these three acts forces each one to face the truth about himself and about his society.

Unlike *A Doll's House*, where there are servants and a sub-plot between Krogstad and Mrs. Linde, only five characters appear in *Ghosts*. No one is included who has not a place in the main action itself. In this way, an atmosphere of austere grandeur is given to the whole drama providing it with an intensity suggestive of classical plays. Professor Koht describes the play's further relationship to ancient drama for Greek tragedy, often called the fate, or family drama, shows a tragic flaw inherited through the generations. *Ghosts* is also a "family tragedy," he writes, "but it is also a social drama—the ancient tragedy resurrected on modern soil."

Captain Alving's character bears this out. The source of the hereditary flaw which destroys his children, his presence pervades each scene of *Ghosts*. As each living character illuminates the nature of the diseased profligate, he finally stands as clearly and as well-drawn to the audience as if he were constantly active on stage. Almost as a "secondary" protagonist, Alving undergoes a change of character until he is presented to the spectator as an individual whom society has wronged. Finally, when Mrs. Alving recognizes how she destroyed his "joy of life," the dead husband is no longer a ghost, but a humanized victim of the social conventions.

CHARACTER ANALYSIS

Pastor Manders

Pastor Manders, simple-minded and self-involved like Torvald Helmer, exists in an imaginary world where people and events conform to his stereotypes. Depositions such as "It is not a wife's part to be her husband's judge" and "We have no right to do anything that will scandalize the community" show how he accepts all the verbal expressions of social principles but is unable to deal with instances where doctrine does not apply. When he states, for instance, "A child should love and honor his father and mother," Mrs. Alving tartly replies, "Don't let us talk in such general terms. Suppose we say: ought Oswald to love and honor Mr. Alving?" To this conflict of principle and reality which she suggests, the reverend has no response. Hypocritical and prideful, Manders' only reaction to the story of Joanna's scandalous marriage to Engstrand is indignation that he was fooled.

Because of the power that his clerical status accords him, Manders is the most destructive creature in the drama. Incapable of spontaneity, devoid of any intellect, he readily sacrifices individual integrity and freedom of expression to maintain empty social standards. The major incident in a life devoted to hypocrisy occurred when Manders persuaded Mrs. Alving to return to her husband. Delighted to show the world his victory over temptation, he neglected Mrs. Alving's plight. His indifference to the needs of the individual sacrificed the love of a sensitive young woman and doomed her to lifelong despair. Although he is a believable figure in the present play, Manders is too much a stereotype. He speaks for all of society and represents its evils.

Mrs. Alving

Mrs. Alving, raised as a dutiful girl to become a dutiful wife and mother, would easily fall in love with the virtuous Manders. Certainly a man with Alving's exuberance and vitality would not be a suitable husband for her. However, desperate circumstances forced Mrs. Alving to reassess the values she was brought up to maintain. Suffering her hard life with Alving, taking over his business, reading and thinking for herself revitalized her static intellect. By the end of the play she is able to recognize that her sanctimoniousness contributed to perverting Alving's joy of life into lechery and drunkenness. This final awakening comes too late: the ghosts of her past education have already destroyed the children in her care, Regina and Oswald.

What makes Mrs. Alving such an interesting character is her inability to take a stand between keeping up appearances and acting out of personal integrity. At the same time she reads controversial literature and regrets the deceit in her past life, she dedicates a town orphanage to preserve the reputation of her dead husband. Although encouraging Oswald to study art and educating Regina to be a gentlewoman, she raises her son to idealize his father and never tells Regina the facts of her origins. No longer deceiving herself as to the truth of Manders' pious generalizations, Mrs. Alving instills these same "ghosts" into the beliefs of her children.

In another sense, the personal tension in Mrs. Alving is based on her imposed feminine weaknesses in a society where only men expect to express themselves aggressively and self-confidently. In this way, Ibsen recalls the feminist sympathy he expressed in *A Doll's House,* and depicts another tragedy where a woman finally asserts her own individuality and intellect after catastrophe.

Oswald Alving

Oswald Alving, although important in the play, is merely a minor character and represents the doomed product of a diseased society. Artistically gifted by having inherited his father's "joy of life," he finds he cannot work at home where the "sun" of self-expression is obscured by the "fog" of duty and social appearances. Fearing that his exuberance and creativity would dissipate, like that of his father, under these circumstances, he wants to leave home with Regina. However Oswald is doomed by a more drastic form of hereditary dissipation; he ends his life in hopeless lunacy, crying vainly for the sun—the symbolic sun of truth, love, and self-expression that he never found among his own people.

Regina

Regina Engstrand is another victim of society's "ghosts" which destroy the "joy of life" in its female members. Limited by her sex and status, she is unable to channel this vitality into a constructive mode of life. Unable to marry into another social level, Regina has no resources with which to face her future other than her own good looks and spirited temperament.

Jacob Engstrand

Jacob Engstrand, made cynical by his experiences as a member of the lower class, preys upon the established society for his maintenance. Using the same tools of hypocrisy and deceit that Pastor Manders accepts as social principles, Engstrand gains in power and prestige. He personifies how Manders' pious idealism degenerates into ruthless self-interest when social principles are applied to denounce individual integrity.

SYMBOLISM

Ibsen's poetic ability enables him to enrich the prose plays with symbols that have broad as well as narrow meanings. Especially allusive is Ibsen's concept of light and darkness. Oswald's last plea for the sun, for instance, sums up his need for the "joy of life" in himself as well as in his work. He needs sunlight in which to paint and he needs illumination on the nature of his father. A pall hangs over the entire landscape of the play; if there is no rain at the moment, the scene outside the window is obscured by mist. The weather finally clears when Mrs. Alving faces the truth, but it is too late. Thrust into darkness, Oswald weakly cries out for the sun. His last monosyllabic plea has a twofold significance: not only symbolizing the "light of truth," it might stand for the morphia powders which would dispel the lingering darkness that enshrouds Oswald's diseased mind.

The fire that destroys the orphange is another symbol of truth. Purifying the institution of deceit, the flames allow Engstrand to receive support for his planned Alving Home. With characteristic irony, Ibsen implies that there is no deceit in raising a brothel to the memory of the late Captain Alving.

The most pervasive symbol, of course, is that of ghosts. The ghosts are worn ideals and principles of law and order so misapplied that they have no actual significance. All the untested maxims and abstract dogma that Manders maintains are ghosts; all the sources of personal cowardice in Mrs. Alving are ghosts. Ghosts are also the lies about the past, perpetrated to the present, which will haunt the future. Finally, ghosts are the actual and symbolic diseases of heredity which destroy the joy of life in the younger, freer generations.

AN ENEMY OF THE PEOPLE

ACT I

Summary

In the home of Dr. Stockmann, Mrs. Stockmann is offering Mr. Billings, an assistant on the local paper, some more food. She thinks she hears the editor, Mr. Hovstad coming, but it is her brother-in-law, the Mayor (or Burgomaster). He is somewhat shocked to see that the Stockmanns have meat for supper. Mr. Hovstad appears and tells the Burgomaster that he is here on business. Dr. Stockmann often writes an article for Mr. Hovstad's liberal paper. The present article Dr. Stockmann is having printed is about the medicinal value of the new baths which are soon to open up in the town. The Burgomaster speaks about the great value of the baths to the town, but he resents the idea that his brother is credited with being the founder of the baths because he himself was responsible for the execution of the plan.

Dr. Stockmann comes in bringing with him another guest, an old friend named Captain Horster. He greets his brother and explains how great it is now to have a job where he can afford to eat meat twice a day and to buy little items. For many years, he has had to live on almost starvation wages, but now that the Burgomaster has gotten him a position with the baths, he is always in good spirits. The Burgomaster wants to know about the new article Dr. Stockmann is publishing, but Dr. Stockmann tells him it isn't to appear until he checks on a few more facts. The Burgomaster knows that the article is about the baths and demands to be told immediately all about it. When Dr. Stockmann refuses, the Burgomaster leaves in anger.

Hovstad comes in and intimates that the Burgomaster left because the crowd was too liberal for him. There is a town election coming soon and Hovstad's liberal paper has not been supporting the Burgomaster. Petra Stockmann comes in from the school where she teaches and tells her father that she has a letter for him. Dr. Stockmann becomes excited and goes immediately to his study to read the letter. His wife explains to the guests that Dr. Stockmann has been waiting every day for a week for some mysterious letter.

Petra tells the group how difficult it is to teach when the little children have to be told so many things that are not true. She would like to open a school of her own. Captain Horster offers her the bottom of his old house which stands empty most of the time, especially since he is about to sail for America. Hovstad thinks she would do better to come over to journalism and asks her if she has finished the translation of the English novel. She promises to have it completed in a short time.

Dr. Stockmann comes back in and is excited about the news he has just received. He thinks he has made a great discovery. He tells them that he has found out that their magnificent, lovely, highly praised baths are nothing more than a poisonous, pestiferous hole. He explains that the pipes are laid too low and all the filth from the tanning mills is infecting the water. He has spent the entire winter investigating the affair and has sent off samples of the water to the university for analysis. The water contains millions of putrefying organic matter called infusoria. These are detrimental to health whether they are used internally or externally. He explains that this was why so many people were sick last summer at the baths. At the time he thought the people brought the disease with them, but now he knows that they became sick from the water. To correct the situation, all of the water pipes will have to be relaid.

Dr. Stockmann explains that the town has often laughed at his ideas and proposals, but now everyone will see that he is not out of his head. He particularly wants Petra to tell her grandfather who has thought Dr. Stockmann was "not quite right." Furthermore, he has prepared a statement for the directors of the baths and is going to send it to the Burgomaster immediately. Hovstad wants to put a short announcement of the discovery in the paper, and it is suggested that the town should do something to honor Dr. Stockmann. Dr. Stockmann thinks, however, that it is a blessing to have served his native town and its citizens.

Commentary

The first act is concerned with providing background information and other matters of exposition. We are not far enough in the play yet to draw definite character personalities. The exposition (i.e., the handling of background material) provides us with the knowledge that Dr. Stockmann has often been on the verge of extreme poverty, that his brother the Burgomaster has obtained a nice post for him with the new baths in the town, that the idea of the baths were originally Dr. Stockmann's, but the Burgomaster took over and directed the building of the baths along lines which Dr. Stockmann did not approve of. Furthermore, we find out that the two brothers have very little in common. The Burgomaster adheres to old and traditional views and Dr. Stockmann is a man of modern and liberal views. At this point, it is suggested that Hovstad is in agreement with Dr. Stockmann and opposed to the Burgomaster but this will later be dramatically reversed.

There are also enough hints in this first act to indicate that Dr. Stockmann is an impulsive man. He writes articles for the newspaper on any new idea he has. He does things impetuously and without consultation. He has had many "crackbrained notions" in the past, and has refused to consult the proper authorities.

Dr. Stockmann is also somewhat naive in thinking that the community will be proud of him for discovering that the baths are poisonous. He fails to realize that as important as the discovery is, it is one which will cause an immense amount of expense and inconvenience. Furthermore, there seems to be some ambiguity in his motivations. We know that he was annoyed at the Burgomaster for refusing to lay the pipes where Dr. Stockmann wanted them. Now that he has found out that the pipes are causing the baths to be poisonous, there is a hint of personal satisfaction in proving the Burgomaster wrong. In fact, his happiness can derive directly from his vindication against the Burgomaster who refused to follow Dr. Stockmann's specification for building the baths.

In the statement that Dr. Stockmann has prepared, the reader must inquire whether this statement is an explanation or an accusation. Dr. Stockmann is somewhat naive and innocent when he thinks that the Burgomaster will be pleased at this discovery.

The act ends on a note of irony. Dr. Stockmann thinks that he is going to be honored as a hero and feels good that he served his town and fellow citizens well. It will be only a short time before he will be declared an enemy of the people.

At the end of the first act, the problem has not yet been fully presented. Now it is only that the baths are unsanitary and the conditions of the baths must be changed or altered.

ACT II

Summary
Dr. Stockmann has his manuscript returned to him with a note from the Burgomaster that they should meet at noontime. Mrs. Stockmann suggests that perhaps he should share the honor with his brother. Dr. Stockmann is willing to share the honor if he can get the thing straightened out.

Old Morton Kiil, the man who adopted and raised Mrs. Stockmann, drops by to inquire if the news is correct. He thinks it is a good trick to play on the Burgomaster. Dr. Stockmann doesn't understand. Morton Kiil asks if these poisonous animals are invisible and then says that the Burgomaster will never fall for such a story as that. But he is angry with the Burgomaster and the town council and hopes that his son-in-law will make them all "eat humble pie." When Hovstad drops by, Morton Kiil wonders if Hovstad is also involved. Now he is convinced that Stockmann and Hovstad are in some conspiracy to make the Burgomaster look foolish.

When old Morton Kiil leaves, Dr. Stockmann is astounded at the possibility that people won't believe him. Hovstad points out that a good many other things are involved aside from the medical aspect. He suggests that the poison comes not just from the tanning mills, but also from the poisonous life that the entire community is living. The "town has gradually drifted into the hands of a pack of bureaucrats," and that is why the pipes were laid in the wrong place to begin with. The leaders of the town show no foresight and no ability. He wants to take up the matter in the paper and use the case of the baths to clear the town council of all the "obstinate old blockheads" who are holding progress back. This is their chance to "emancipate the downtrodden masses."

Aslaksen, the printer, appears and offers his support to Dr. Stockmann. He is the head of the "compact majority in the town" and is sure the compact majority will stand behind Dr. Stockmann. He is thinking of some type of demonstration if one could be held with moderation. Dr. Stockmann explains that he needs no support because the issues are so clear and self-evident. But Aslaksen reminds him that the authorities always move slowly.

After Aslaksen leaves, Hovstad insists that "this gross, inexcusable blunder of the water-works must be brought home clearly to every voter." Dr. Stockmann asks him to wait until he can consult with his brother. After Hovstad leaves, Dr. Stockmann tells his family how good it feels to be able to do something good for his town.

The Burgomaster comes in to discuss the baths with Dr. Stockmann. He asks Dr. Stockmann if he checked to see how much new pipes would cost and how long it would take. They would cost around sixty thousand dollars and would take two years to relay. In the meantime, the baths would have to be closed down and after word got around that they were poisonous, no one would ever come to them anymore and the town would be literally bankrupt. He tells Dr. Stockmann that his report will literally ruin the town and that Dr. Stockmann will be responsible for the total destruction of his own town. Dr. Stockmann is shocked, but says that the baths are still contaminated and something must be done. The Burgomaster, however, is not convinced that the condition is as serious as Dr.

Stockmann says it is. He accuses his brother of exaggerating greatly, and suggests that a competent physician should be able to do something to rectify the situation. But Dr. Stockmann asserts that anything short of relaying the pipes would be dishonest: it would be "a fraud, a lie, an absolute crime against the public, against society as a whole." He believes it is just stubbornness and fear of blame that keeps the Burgomaster from recognizing the disastrous state of the baths. Dr. Stockmann reminds the Burgomaster that the plan of the baths was "bungled" by the authorities, and now these same people cannot admit they were wrong. The Burgomaster reminds Dr. Stockmann that as an individual he has no right to an individual opinion and must always rely on the authorities. He therefore forbids Dr. Stockmann to turn in his report or to meddle any further in the affairs of the baths. Furthermore, he demands that Dr. Stockmann obey him. But the doctor says he will take his case to the papers and will write against the Burgomaster: he will prove that the "source is poisoned" and that the people "live by trafficking in filth and corruption. The whole of our flourishing social life is rooted in a lie."

The Burgomaster warns Dr. Stockmann that such "offensive insinuations against his native place" will brand him as an enemy of society. After the Burgomaster leaves, Dr. Stockmann is proud to know that he has the independent press and the compact majority behind him. He is determined to carry out his plan. Mrs. Stockmann reminds him that he has a family to look after and they might suffer dire consequences. Dr. Stockmann, however, feels that he must stand by his principles or he would never "have the right to look my boys in the face."

Commentary

Act I only presented the need of the baths to be cleansed. Act II begins to develop the problem with more implications. We are now able to see that the play is going to handle the broad subject of *private* vs. *public* morality. Or as the problem will later be developed, the conflict between *personal integrity* and *social obligation*. This idea will be more fully developed in later acts.

This act presents our first hint of the public's refusal to believe Stockmann. It comes from Stockmann's father-in-law. He believes that Dr. Stockmann is slyly trying to avenge himself against his brother by making the Burgomaster and the entire town council admit that they made a tremendous mistake. If Dr. Stockmann can do that, old Morton Kiil will be happy because they had previously forced him off the town council.

With the appearance of Hovstad, we see the liberal who is ready to jump at any cause and champion that cause as long as he thinks the cause will be popular and will increase circulation.

With Aslaksen, we see the man of cautious good will. He wants to do everything with moderation and not offend anyone. He represents the "compact majority"—that group of people who have no opinions and who follow others like a herd of animals.

When the Burgomaster appears, Dr. Stockmann is shocked to find out that his proposal will cost so much and will take so long to effect. The Burgomaster then is seen as a practical man who believes that the men in authority should decide everything. His view is that the individual freedom should be subjected to the demands of the authorities. This is, of course, a legitimate view, but Ibsen does not leave it a clash between two opposing ideological views. The Burgomaster's views must be seen in terms of his personal involvement. If the news of the baths is made public, he as the authority will be seen to have made a mistake. This will be a personal slight. But also, if the news of the baths is made public, the town will suffer tremendous losses and will be virtually destroyed; thus, his duty as the chief magistrate of the town is to try to save the town. Thus as was Dr. Stockmann's discovery tainted by his desire to avenge himself against the authorities, so now is the Burgomaster's defense somewhat tinged with personal motives.

Dr. Stockmann is still seen as somewhat the impractical visionary. He can see nothing except that the baths are dangerous and poisonous. It may be suggested that he is so confident in his views since he knows (or thinks) that the press and the compact majority are behind him. And under all circumstances, he is a man who does believe strongly in personal freedom and will not submit blindly to the rule of the authorities.

Mrs. Stockmann is seen in this scene as the eternal matriarch; that is, she is the eternal mother and wife figure whose main concern is with the personal welfare of her immediate family.

At the end of the act, we find that perhaps the town will consider Dr. Stockmann an enemy of the society. This is, of course, ironic because Dr. Stockmann thought he was doing a great service to the community. It is his desire to serve his fellow man that hurts more than anything else. Unlike the Burgomaster who believes that the people are like a herd and not worthy of consideration, Dr. Stockmann here believes in the potential capabilities of all the people and counts strongly on the general public to see his point of view.

ACT III

Summary

In the editor's room of the "People's Messenger," Hovstad and his assistant, Billing, are discussing Dr. Stockmann's article. They feel that now the Burgomaster is in trouble and they will use this trouble to hound him out of office. They hope to replace him with men of more "liberal ideas."

Dr. Stockmann arrives and tells the men to go ahead with the publication of his article. They call Aslaksen who wants to know if the article will offend people. He is assured that all intelligent and prudent men will support the article. Dr. Stockmann believes that his article will send all the old bunglers packing, and the town will have a new regime. Aslaksen insists that they proceed with moderation. He explains that he has learned caution when attacking local authorities. If it is a subject of attacking the national government, he is not timid, but with local authorities, one must proceed with caution. Billing maintains that Dr. Stockmann will be declared "a Friend of the People."

After Dr. Stockmann and Aslaksen leave, Hovstad wishes that they could get some financial backing from someone else so that they wouldn't have to rely on Aslaksen. They think about old Morton Kiil who is bound to have some money and the money will go to Dr. Stockmann's family. At this time, Petra comes in to explain that she refuses to translate a certain English novel because it does not conform with Hovstad's liberal ideas. The novel is unrealistic and false to life. Hovstad explains that the paper must print something to attract the attention of the reader so as to trap him into reading the more important liberal ideas. Petra feels this is not honorable and is somewhat disgusted. In further discussions, Petra sees that Hovstad is "not the man" he pretended to be, and she tells him that she will never trust him again.

As Petra leaves, Aslaksen comes in to tell Hovstad that the Burgomaster is in the printing office. After some small talk, the Burgomaster sees Dr. Stockmann's article. He wants to know if the paper is going to print and support Dr. Stockmann's position. He inquires about the compact majority and pretends to be surprised that so many of the "poorer class appear to be so heroically eager to make sacrifices." Aslaksen and Hovstad are confused. The Burgomaster explains that it will require this huge sum of money, which will have to come from the town, and the project will take two years to complete. In the meantime, other towns will take over the business and when the news reaches other places, no one will ever come to their town. Hovstad and Aslaksen now see that Dr. Stockmann was not informed of all the facts. The Burgomaster explains that he is not convinced that there is anything wrong with the water supply. He has brought with him a short statement of what should be done about the baths and wonders if the paper will care to print it.

Just as Hovstad is accepting the paper, they see Dr. Stockmann approaching. The Burgomaster hides in the next room. Dr. Stockmann asks if the first proofs on his article are ready. He is told it will be quite some time. He warns his friends not to get up any type of testimonial for him because it would be too embarrassing. Mrs. Stockmann comes in and warns her husband of the trouble he is getting the entire family into. At this time, Dr. Stockmann notices the Burgomaster's hat and cane. He routs his brother out of hiding and tells him that the power has now changed hands. But Aslaksen and Hovstad take the Burgomaster's side. Both explain that Dr. Stockmann's plan will ruin the town. Dr. Stockmann refuses to budge from his position. He maintains that the truth cannot be killed by a "conspiracy of silence." He promises that his report will be made public in spite of all threats. As the men turn against Dr. Stockmann, his wife comes to his side and promises to stand by him always. He is told he can have no hall to speak in and no society will listen to him. He threatens to stand on the street corner and read his paper to the people.

Commentary

Act III is the changing point in the drama. Here we see the various motives of the characters examined under pressures and thus we find out who are the real men of principles. At the first of the act when Aslaksen and Hovstad think that the doctor's discovery will be popular and beneficial and when they think it will provide an opportunity to get rid of the old authorities, they are supporting him. Later when they realize that it will be harmful to the town and therefore unpopular, they turn against the doctor. Aslaksen is a man who does not wish to offend anyone and who wants to proceed with moderation. But more important, when his principles are confronted with the possibility that he will lose financially, the principles are no longer important.

With Hovstad, we see in his discussion with Petra, that he is not a man of true principles. He publishes not what he believes in but what he thinks will increase circulation. Thus his allegiance to Dr. Stockmann stems not from a belief in the truth of Dr. Stockmann's ideas, but from the hope that his cause will be a popular one and thus increase circulation.

With the appearance of the Burgomaster, the theme of personal integrity and social obligation becomes dominant. The Burgomaster is attempting to save the town, but in doing so, he is also trying to preserve his image as the town's foremost citizen. If the report is made public, it will destroy both the town and the Burgomaster's reputation because he was responsible for the construction of the water pipes which cause all the trouble. Thus for the benefit of the town and his own personal integrity, he refuses to believe the truth of Dr. Stockmann's report and hints that the doctor has always been impetuous and wild in his ideas.

Dr. Stockmann is now seen as the impractical idealist. In striving to achieve the ideal or the perfectly moral solution, he ignores all practical advice and opposes everyone who would stand in his way. In other words, he is ready to carry his idealism to absurd degrees.

Mrs. Stockmann is somewhat comic in these scenes. She is opposed to her husband's plans until the people turn against him. Then she is ready to stand by him simply because he is her husband. She doesn't understand what is at stake here, but is nevertheless convinced that her husband is right even though a few moments earlier she was trying to get him to change.

ACT IV

Summary

In the large bottom room of Captain Horster's house, there is to be a meeting. It is heard that Dr. Stockmann was unable to find another meeting place and his old friend offered him this place. The citizens gathering are wondering what they should do. They decide to watch Aslaksen and do as he does. Dr. Stockmann and his family arrive and the Burgomaster comes in from another direction. Hovstad and Billing are also there.

Before Dr. Stockmann can start his speech, the Burgomaster and Aslaksen insist that a chairman be elected. Dr. Stockmann points out that it is unnecessary since he only wants to give a lecture. But a chairman is elected. It is Aslaksen. Then the Burgomaster moves that the meeting decline to hear the lecture on the subject of the baths. After more speeches and confusion, Dr. Stockmann tells the audience that he does not wish to speak on the subject of the baths but on something entirely different. He is allowed to begin.

The theme of Dr. Stockmann's speech is that the "sources of our spiritual life are poisoned, and that our whole society rests upon a pestilential basis of falsehood." He then attacks the leading men who act like goats and do harm at every point. They block the path of a free man and are filled with prejudices. But more dangerous is the compact majority. The country should be run by the intelligent men and since the majority is made up of fools, it should have no right to a voice in the government. He proves that with animals only the thoroughbreds are worth anything. The same should be true with people. The herd of men are no better than curs, and should be kept in that position.

At this point the crowd begins to revolt. A motion is made to declare Dr. Stockmann an enemy of the people. The motion is passed with only one person voting against it. Old Morton Kiil comes to Stockmann and wonders if the poison comes from his tannery as well as the others. Dr. Stockmann tells him that the Morton Kiil Tannery is one of the worst and will have to be improved immediately. Old Morton Kiil tells Stockmann that such an accusation may cost the Stockmann family a lot of money.

Dr. Stockmann asks Captain Horster if he has room on his ship for the Stockmanns to sail with him to America. Captain Horster tells him that he will make room.

Commentary

The act opens with Stockmann still convinced that he is working for the sake of the people. Thinking that he will now become the champion of the people, he obtains a hall in order to give a lecture. Thus, this act pits the idealist against the common herd of people, the people whom Stockmann wants to serve.

Apparently, Stockmann wanted to give his speech about the baths. But the democratic principles of electing a chairman for the committee and then entertaining a motion as to whether Dr. Stockmann should be heard changed the nature of the speech. He therefore delivers a tirade against the democratic processes and attempts to prove that the common man has no business having a voice in the government. He is, of course, still the idealist, but here the idealist is trapped in the involved processes of bureaucracy. He sees his idealism being defeated by the very people he wanted to help; thus, he attacks the people and the officials elected by the officials.

The reader must realize that Stockmann's speech is offensive. But he remains a sympathetic character because the purpose of his speech is noble. He is striving to realize his ideals without compromising his principles. Everyone else at the meeting has in one way or another compromised himself — has sold out for personal gain or to avoid a difficult conflict. But in his attack, we must step back and realize that Dr. Stockmann has carried idealism to its extreme.

The question arises then: Is Dr. Stockmann an enemy of the people? If we were to isolate Dr. Stockmann's speech, that is, take it out of the context of all that went before, and if we were to hear only what the audience at Dr. Stockmann's speech heard, then we would see that Dr. Stockmann's present position is one that justifies his being called an enemy of the people. He has openly advocated that the people are not capable of voting correctly. He has insulted the common people and has referred to them in terms of a herd of animals. Thus, by this speech alone, Dr. Stockmann is an enemy of the people. But actually, we know that his attack is motivated by more noble reasons and only in his disillusionment does he make such heavy charges against the very people he wants to help.

ACT V

Summary

Dr. Stockmann's home is in disorder. He appears holding a stone which someone cast through his window. He wants to save it as a reminder of his days of persecution. He receives a letter from the landlord giving him notice to move. Petra arrives from the school and tells her family that she has been dismissed. All of this is because the people are afraid to go against the popular opinion. Captain Horster comes in and tells them that he has lost his ship because the owner is afraid of popular opinion. Next the Burgomaster arrives and hands Dr. Stockmann his dismissal from the baths. The Burgomaster tells Dr. Stockmann that a circular is being sent around advising people not to engage Dr. Stockmann. He suggests to Dr. Stockmann that he could be reinstated in a couple of months if he would write a document saying that all of his ideas about the baths were false. But Dr. Stockmann refuses.

The Burgomaster accuses Doctor Stockmann of acting so highly because he knows of old Morton Kiil's will. But Dr. Stockmann knows nothing. The Burgomaster tells him that old Morton Kiil is wealthy and is leaving a large portion of his fortune to Dr. Stockmann's children and that he and Mrs. Stockmann are to have the "life-interest" on it. Dr. Stockmann is tremendously relieved to know that his wife and children are taken care of. The Burgomaster accuses Dr. Stockmann of creating all the trouble simply because Old Morton Kiil has a quarrel with the town council. Dr. Stockmann is almost speechless and calls his wife to scrub the floor where the Burgomaster walked out.

Shortly, Old Morton Kiil comes to call upon Dr. Stockmann. He explains that he has been out buying up shares of the baths with the money which he was to leave Mrs. Stockmann and the children. He feels that his tannery is the cause of the foulness in the water and he wants Stockmann to clear the Morton Kiil name. Thus, if Dr. Stockmann continues in his insistence upon the destructive element involved in the baths, then he is cutting off his own family from a large inheritance. Dr. Stockmann is stunned, and says he will talk to his wife. After all, the people have turned against him and he can do very little. He is to let Morton Kiil know by two o'clock.

As Morton Kiil is leaving, Hovstad and Aslaksen arrive. They immediately ask Dr. Stockmann if his father-in-law hasn't been buying stocks in the baths. Then they suggest it would have been more prudent of Dr. Stockmann to have let them in on his little plan of secretly buying up the baths stocks after giving out the false rumors. This is too much for Dr. Stockmann. He grabs his stick and drives both men out of the house. He calls Petra and sends his answer immediately to Old Morton Kiil. He then tells his wife that they will stay in the town and fight all the worse elements. He will found a school and teach the street curs how to think and act properly. He has, he says, learned one great lesson—the strongest man is the man who stands alone.

Commentary

Act V is a practical or materialistic test of Dr. Stockmann's idealism. In the last act, we saw Aslaksen and Hovstad retract when they stood to lose something personally. This act now confronts Dr.

Stockmann with great personal losses if he continues to assert his views. This test is necessary before we can formulate a complete view of Dr. Stockmann.

Before he faces his test, he first learns that his views have caused Captain Horster to lose his ship and Petra to lose her position in the school. Furthermore he has faced his own dismissal from the baths. Thus when Old Morton Kiil comes to him asking him to retract his charges or else all of his inheritance will go to charity, Dr. Stockmann is about ready to yield to the public opinion. He is prevented by the appearance of Hovstad and Aslaksen. When Dr. Stockmann sees that he can gain the admiration of his fellow townsmen by admitting that he engineered the entire plan so as to gain control of the stock of the baths, this accusation (or this admiration) is worse than the rejection by the people. He therefore decides to stand by his idealistic views.

Finally we must note that Dr. Stockmann's idealism is not consistent. In Act IV he denied that the common curs could be of any value to society. But in Act V, he says he is going to take the common "street-curs" and educate them into the leading men of society who will then drive out all the bureaucrats. His saving factor, however, is his strong belief in that which is right.

GENERAL ANALYSIS

STRUCTURE AND TECHNIQUE

As with most problem plays, *An Enemy of the People* takes a specific situation and uses it to make a larger general statement about mankind. Here we have the specific problem of the bad water pipes at the new health baths. The question then is simply one of cleaning the baths. It is a matter of civic health and sanitation. From this specific situation, Ibsen then moves to the more complex problem of private versus public morality. Or to state it in other words, Ibsen is investigating the relationship between moral and ethical responsibility when seen against practical exigency.

To present this problem, Ibsen creates an idealist in the person of Dr. Stockmann and has him diametrically opposed by his own brother who is the man of extreme practicality. In other words, Dr. Stockmann represents private and public morality while his brother, the Burgomaster, represents the practical aspect of life.

The problem which perplexes many readers of this play is Ibsen's apparent failure to make his position clear. But this was not Ibsen's purpose. He is not offering a stated solution to his problem, but instead, he is presenting a full measured discussion of the problem. The sensible man would assume a position somewhere between that of Dr. Stockmann and the Burgomaster. In his idealism, Dr. Stockmann forgets that the world moves by practical means. It is revealed early in the play that Dr. Stockmann conceived the idea of the baths but could never bring them to a practical completion. It took the Burgomaster to do that. Thus, Dr. Stockmann is seen essentially as a comic figure whose idealism blinds him to the commonplace practicality of the world. But the Burgomaster is equally as blinded to the ethical questions of the world. Therefore, after a thorough consideration of the ideas, the reader should take a stand somewhere between the two extremes represented by the main characters.

CHARACTER ANALYSIS

Aslaksen

Aslaksen is the man of cautious good will. His constant comment involves "proceeding with moderation." He is afraid of offending anyone who is in authority, unless that person is some distant abstract person who cannot immediately affect him. He represents the compact majority who believes in civic progress so long as it does not involve any expense or effort. He is the type who would rather suffer any type of bad situation rather than get involved in a drastic change.

Hovstad

Hovstad is the professional type of liberal who constantly wants to stir things up as long as he is not directly involved and will not be personally affected. His main concern is to increase the circulation of his paper, and for this purpose he will ignore any principle.

He supports Dr. Stockmann as long as he thinks the compact majority and the public are behind Dr. Stockmann. But as soon as it is known that the public will not support any idea which is going to cost money, he turns against Dr. Stockmann and supports the Burgomaster.

Mrs. Stockmann

She is a minor character who represents the eternal matriarch. Her interest is in the family. She does not care for civic causes, but when her husband is attacked by other people, she comes to his side even though she does not understand the principles behind the cause.

Peter Stockmann, (The Burgomaster)

The Burgomaster represents the old established order of things. He believes that authority should rest in the hands of the officials and that all individuals should be subjected to the rule of these authorities. He does not believe in personal or individual expressions. He is convinced that he is right and anyone opposed to him must be wrong. He tells Dr. Stockmann that "the individual must subordinate himself to society, or, more precisely, to the authorities whose business it is to watch over the welfare of society." He is, then, the reactionary who is afraid of any change because change implies a reevaluation of authority.

The Burgomaster is not a man of strong ethical principles. Instead, he is the practical man who looks to see how something will bring a practical or material reward. He cannot conceive of the possibility that he might be wrong in anything. Thus part of his opposition to Dr. Stockmann's news about the baths is due to the fact that the Burgomaster was responsible for placing the water-pipes in the wrong place. He is incapable of facing the fact that he made a tremendous error, and therefore, he must repress the news of the bad sanitary conditions so that his own reputation will be preserved.

Dr. Stockmann

Dr. Stockmann represents the extreme idealist who has no concept of the practical side of life. His idealism blinds him to the common procedures of everyday activity.

As an idealist, Dr. Stockmann believes strongly in individual freedom and the right of every man to express himself freely. He cannot become a party to any dishonest or unethical act. Thus, he cannot bend in any sense of the word. He is accurately characterized as too impetuous. As soon as he finds out about the bad sanitary conditions at the baths, he immediately makes the news public and refuses to listen to any compromise and demands that the water pipes be relaid. He does not try to convince the people of his view, but instead, goes directly and blindly at a demanded improvement. It is, therefore, his lack of tact and understanding of the practical issues which place him in such an awkward position.

There is, however, a touch of jealous revenge in Dr. Stockmann's actions. He was annoyed that the Burgomaster did not build the pipes according to the doctor's original specifications, and thus he is delighted that he is able to prove the Burgomaster to be wrong.

Furthermore, Dr. Stockmann's idealism is somewhat muddled. He is not consistent. At one point he maintains that the common people have no right to a voice in the government. But this is what the Burgomaster had previously told the doctor and the doctor had stoutly asserted the right of every citizen to express his own views. Likewise, he suggests that the common people are like curs or impure animals and can never be educated to take a significant role in the development of a society. Yet at the end he is going to take some "street-curs" and educate them to run the wolves out of the government.

Dr. Stockmann is saved as a character because he puts his principles above his own desires and gains. He is not tempted by financial rewards enough to deny the truth of the condition of the baths. He is thoroughly disgusted by the petty and dishonest interpretations placed on his actions. And as a man of great personal integrity, he spurns a large inheritance in order to maintain an ethical and moral responsibility to himself and to his community.

THE WILD DUCK

INTRODUCTION

As in previous plays, Ibsen uses his "retrospective technique" which, in the words of George Brandes, a contemporary critic, "is the principle of advancing by going backwards to the revelations of the past." The characters in *The Wild Duck* are related through complicated events in their past history, and, for the sake of efficiency, these relationships are outlined under "Character Analysis."

ACT I

Summary

Mr. Werle is giving a party in honor of his son's homecoming. Besides influential political friends, he has also invited Hialmar Ekdal, an old schoolfellow of Gregers. Feeling out of place and uncomfortable among the guests, Hialmar is more gloomy than ever when he overhears Werle whisper to Gregers that he hopes none noticed that they were thirteen at table. His friend however reassures him; feeling more alien in his father's house than Hialmar feels, Gregers avers that he himself is "the thirteenth."

In another room, the servants reluctantly admit Old Ekdal. He explains that he has come to fetch some copy work which the book-keeper left for him, and, unseen by the guests, he steals into the office.

Conversing with his old friend, Gregers is surprised to learn that Hialmar has married their former maidservant. Gina is a different person than the one he knew as a servant, young Ekdal explains; "she is by no means without culture" for "life itself is an education." He boasts that "her daily intercourse with me" has refined her "and then we know one or two rather remarkable men who come a good deal about us."

Thronging into the room, the chamberlains are joking with Mrs. Sorby who keeps up the witty repartee. Gregers advises his friend to join the conversation, but Hialmar does not know what to say. During a discussion about wines, he makes the guests laugh by asking whether vintages differ according to their seasons. As Werle involuntarily exclaims "Ugh," the guests turn to see the shabbily dressed Lieutenant Ekdal walk with the bookkeeper to the front door. Hialmar turns his back and faces the fireplace. When asked whether he knew that man, the son stammers "I don't know—I didn't notice" while Gregers recovers from his shock at old Ekdal's appearance. Reproaching Hialmar, young Werle says, "And you could stand there and deny that you knew him!" but the loudness of the guests interrupts their further conversation.

When Werle has a chance for a private talk with his son, Gregers shows deep bitterness toward his father. Accusing Werle of deceit in marrying off Gina to Hialmar, reproaching the lecherous behavior which caused his mother's death, Gregers concludes by blaming his father for ruining old Ekdal's life by framing him for the government swindle. Werle denies this last accusation. He tells his son that he should bury his past grievances and show filial approval for the intended marriage to Mrs. Sorby. It is not fair to his future wife to be a spectacle of scandal, and besides, they are well suited to each other. Gregers laughs scornfully. Never was there any family life in this house, he says, and now for the sake of Mrs. Sorby we are to set up a pretense of harmony, a "tableau of filial affection" to annihilate the last rumors "as to the wrongs the dead mother had to submit to." Pitying the gullibility of "poor Hialmar Ekdal" who does not realize that "what he calls his home is built up on a lie," Gregers says he will leave the house forever "for at last I see my mission in life."

Commentary

Despite the brevity of this act, it lacks the intensity and tension that the introductory scenes build up in the previous plays. Ibsen quickly establishes all the relationships, however, and as he develops the history of his characters he shows which ones are "realistic" (old Werle and Mrs. Sorby, for instance) and which ones are tainted with "idealism" to cover their own weaknesses (Gregers and Hialmar Ekdal).

Mrs. Sorby appears in this act as a woman of the world. Although without status, she is able to treat her influential guests as equals and behaves with frankness (wittily implying that the chamberlains take graft) and compassion (ordering the servant to give "something nice" to old Ekdal to take home).

Hialmar Ekdal exposes his concern for keeping up appearances. At the same time he mourns his father's fallen position in society, he refuses to acknowledge publicly that he is related to the disreputable old man who intrudes on the high class party. Insisting that his wife is "not without education" Hialmar shows his status-seeking aspirations and proves that he has an inflated self-conceit.

The appearance of Lieutenant Ekdal at the party shows the audience his simplicity and lack of self-consciousness. He seems a creature from another world who merely stumbles blindly through those social spheres which include the chamberlains, Mr. Werle, and Mrs. Sorby. According to this scheme, Gregers and Hialmar, who each suspect themselves of being "thirteenth at table," inhabit a peripheral sphere which lies somewhere between the worlds of old Ekdal and old Werle.

ACT II

Summary

The scene takes place in Ekdal's studio. Gina is sewing; her daughter Hedvig peers at a book on the table. They talk desultorily, recounting the costs of food items, the major part of their budget going for butter and beer. Their conversation shows how frugally they live, keeping luxury items for Hialmar's consumption and sacrificing their own cravings for delicacies. Hedvig hopes her father will return soon, for he promised to bring her "something nice" to eat from the dinner party.

When Lieutenant Ekdal returns with a package under his arm and asks no one to disturb him in his room this evening, mother and daughter exchange knowing smiles; they realize the old man intends to spend the evening with his cognac. Hialmar appears and his father emerges to greet him. While the women eagerly help him take his overcoat, they admire how handsome he looks and ask many questions about the party. Hialmar names the guests he consorted with—"Chamberlain Flor and Chamberlain Balle and Chamberlain Kaspersen"—and they are all very impressed. Carried away by his sense of importance, Ekdal represents himself as the most intellectual and vivacious man at the party. He concludes by treating his family to a lecture about the vintages of wine.

Hedvig expectantly eyes her father, but he has not the slightest idea at what she is hinting. Finally she asks him to bring forth the good things he promised. Hialmar confesses that he forgot all about it. "But wait, Hedvig, I do have something for you," he says digging in his pockets while she jumps up and down in happy anticipation. To her disappointment, he brings out the menu, announcing he will read the bill of fare and describe all the rich dishes to her. Seeing how she gulps back her tears, he interrupts his menu reading, angrily complaining about "the absurd things the father of a family is expected to think of" and being treated to "sour faces" when he forgets the smallest trifle.

The wife and daughter dutifully change the subject, but Hialmar still feels like a martyr. To further fill "his cup of bitterness," Ekdal supposes that no one has yet rented their spare room, and he supposes that no new customers have shown up for portrait sittings, and, sighing, concludes he is willing to work "so long as my strength holds out." Hedvig humbly offers him some beer. Waving her away, he says, "I require nothing, nothing." Adding at once "Beer? Was it beer you were talking about?" Hialmar accepts and all four are happy again. Glass in hand, surrounded by his family, Ekdal pronounces his forgiveness. "Our roof may be poor and humble, but it is home," he says. "And with all my heart I say: Here dwells my happiness."

There is a knock on the door, and Gina admits Gregers Werle. During their talk, Hialmar lowers his voice to prevent Hedvig from hearing. The child is in danger of losing her eyesight, he informs Gregers, although only the first symptoms have appeared as yet. The blindness will inexorably develop, for it is a hereditary disease. "Yes," Gina quickly avers, "Ekdal's mother had weak eyes," but Gregers is suspicious.

Gregers turns to greet Lieutenant Ekdal, reminding the old man how he used to be an avid hunter in the days when he worked in the forests. "How can a man like you—such a man for the open air— live in the midst of a stuffy town, boxed within four walls?" asks Gregers. In reply, Ekdal draws young Werle to the door of the garret where skylights admit beams of moonlight to illuminate the darkness of a large room. Proudly the old man shows his guest the barely discernible pigeons, rabbits, especially pointing out their favorite treasure asleep in a basket—a wild duck. Quietly closing the door, old Ekdal tells Gregers that the wild duck was an indirect present from his father, for Werle brought it back wounded from a hunting trip and had asked a servant to get rid of it. After the duck had been shot, Werle's "amazingly clever dog" dived to retrieve it from the depths of the lake:

> They always do that, wild ducks do [continues the old man]. They dive to the bottom as deep as they can get, sir—and bite themselves fast in the tangle and seaweed. And they never come up again.

She thrives wonderfully well in the garret, Hialmar proudly relates. By now the wild duck is so used to it that she has forgotten her natural wild life and "it all depends on that." Nodding, Gregers counsels them to "be sure you never let her get a glimpse of the sky and the sea" for then she will pine for her former freedom.

He surprises them by asking if he may rent their spare room. Hialmar agrees and asks what Gregers plans to do in town:

> I should like best to be an amazingly clever dog [answers young Werle], one that goes to the bottom after wild ducks when they dive and bite themselves fast in tangle and seaweed down among the ooze.

Gregers bids them good-night, proposing to move in the next morning. Old Ekdal has fallen asleep by this time and Gina and Hialmar carry him to bed as the curtain falls.

Commentary

In the first act, Ibsen describes the world of Hakon Werle. Not only does the transition to the setting of the second scene provide interesting contrast with the wealthy industrialist's circle, but it implies that Hialmar Ekdal's household is a direct offspring of old Werle's achievements. The Ekdal ménage is possible only because Werle subsidized Ekdal's professional training, provided Hialmar with a wife and child, and even furnished the precious wild duck. This relationship between the two worlds—that of old Werle and that of Hialmar—is significant for it underscores the imitative nature of Hialmar Ekdal's life.

More specifically, the important discovery the audience makes in this act about Hialmar's character is his relationship to Hedvig. Feeling deep love for her father, the child believes he is the great man he pretends to be. However Hialmar is too self-involved to return this love. When he tries to compensate Hedvig's disappointment by presenting her with a bill of fare from the dinner party rather than bringing her a promised tidbit from the table, Hialmar symbolizes his entire way of life. The menu as a substitute for the food, represents how Ekdal substitutes high-sounding phrases for a depth of feeling he cannot achieve.

Having established this point, Ibsen now feels his audience is ready to accept the wild duck, and he introduces the bird as a symbol which gains in complexity as the drama develops. In the first place, the wild duck represents the world of fantasy through which Hialmar and his father compensate for the drabness and mediocrity of their lives. She is the final touch, which, like a work of art that requires at least one realistic detail to make it appear real, brings their hunting ground in the garret to a state of perfection. Gregers, however, has a different interpretation of the wild duck myth. He believes that the bird symbolizes the entire Ekdal family who will drown in the ooze of fantasy and self-delusion. He feels it is his mission to rescue the Ekdals from these dangerous depths, just as his father's dog retrieved the duck from the suffocating seaweed.

56

ACT III

Summary

It is late the next morning. Gina describes to her husband the havoc Gregers caused in his room. When he tried to put out the fire in the stove, he poured water on it, flooding the whole floor. She leaves him alone to work on retouching photographs. Ekdal's task is constantly interrupted by his father who discusses needed improvements in the garret. Such jobs as moving the watering trough and cutting a path to the duck's basket interest Hialmar, and he is tempted to leave his work. Seeing his divided attention, Hedvig offers to do the retouching for him, even though it might strain her eyes. Hialmar is overcome by the temptation, and he hands her the brush and proofs and joins his father in the attic.

Gregers enters and asks the child many questions. Hedvig informs him that her eyes are now too weak for her to attend school and Hialmar has promised to read with her at home, although he has never had time yet. Gregers also makes Gina uncomfortable by his searching questions. She is forced to admit that she carries on most of the business for her husband; besides having learned to retouch, she also takes the photographs. "You can't expect a man like Ekdal to do nothing but take pictures of Dick, Tom, and Harry," she says. "He's not like one of your common photographers." They hear a shot fired in the garret, and Hialmar emerges, embarrassed when Gregers remarks that "you have become a sportsman, too." Ekdal snappishly replies that he does "a little rabbit shooting now and then, mostly to please father, you understand."

Hialmar asks his wife to prepare lunch. Besides Gregers, he has invited Molvik and Relling, the clergyman and physician who live downstairs, to eat with them. Turning to Gregers, Hialmar now divulges why he leaves the "everyday business details" to Gina: he must "give his mind" to more important things — an invention that will "so exalt" photography that it will become both "an art and a science." It is not for his own sake, he continues, that he pursues this sacred mission. Through his invention he will restore his father's reputation by "restoring the name of Ekdal to honor and dignity." He can give no details about the nature of his invention as yet, but he spends time thinking about it—such work cannot be rushed nor can one be goaded to it, he says. "I almost think you have something of the wild duck in you," Gregers tells him. You have strayed into a "poisonous marsh" and now that "insidious disease has taken hold of you, you have sunk down to die in the dark."

Relling and Molvik arrive just as lunch is ready. The physician remembers Gregers from the Höidal works. "He went around to all the cottars' cabins presenting something he called 'the claim of the ideal,'" Relling tells the company. He wonders whether Gregers has become less idealistic over the years. "Never when I have a true man to deal with," young Werle answers fervently. Changing the subject, Relling cheerfully announces that Molvik was disgustingly drunk the night before. He is demonic, you know, the doctor explains, "and demonic natures are not made to walk straight through the world; they must meander a little now and then."

As they dine, Hialmar makes a maudlin little speech about his devotion to Hedvig and tells Gina she is a "good helpmate on the path of life." Relling turns to Gregers remarking how pleasant to sit at a "well-spread table in a happy family circle." For my part, answers Werle, "I don't thrive in marsh vapors," and Gina is insulted for she gives the house a good airing every day. "No airing you can give will drive out the taint I mean," says Gregers and he leaves the table.

At a sudden knock at the door, old Mr. Werle enters, asking to speak with his son. After everyone discreetly departs, Werle informs Gregers that, with his marriage, his son's share of the property falls to him. Gregers refuses to accept the money; he wants for nothing, he says, and has only his "mission" to fulfill. He wants to cut all ties with his father.

After Werle leaves, Gregers asks Hialmar to join him for a long walk. Dr. Relling bitterly sees them go. "It's a thousand pities the fellow didn't go to hell through one of the Höidal mines," he says aloud. Gina remarks that Werle must be mad; his only disease, says Relling, is an "acute attack of integrity."

Commentary

The significant feature of this act is that it establishes the points of opposition between Relling and Gregers. Both men feel responsible for the lives of others, but the physician's "mission" is contrary to that of Gregers. Ibsen shows that the realist is the one who encourages self-deception as a technique of facing life's disappointments (Relling provides Hialmar with an approving audience for Ekdal's empty pronouncements) while the idealist encourages truthfulness as a way to self-fulfillment.

ACT IV

Summary

It is later in the afternoon, and Gina and Hedvig wonder where Hialmar is. Dinner is late, a feature unusual in the Ekdal home. Finally Hialmar arrives, looking tired and worn. They think he is ill because he refuses to eat. He increases their anxiety by announcing that from now on he shall begin to take all the work in his own hands. What about the invention, asks Gina. Hedvig implores, "And think about the wild duck, father, and all the hens and rabbits." He will never set foot in that garret again, Hialmar says; "I should almost like to wring that cursed wild duck's neck!" Hedvig covers her ears. "Oh no, father, you know it's my wild duck," she cries and shakes him. For her sake, Hialmar promises, he shall never harm the bird. After Hedvig goes for her afternoon walk, the husband and wife are able to talk.

Questioning Gina, Hialmar forces her to admit of her previous liaison with old Werle. She was afraid to tell him before their marriage, Gina says, for fear he would change his mind. Now that their home is cozy and happy, more money comes in every day, they can forget about past happenings, she tells him. "This dull callous contentment," rails Hialmar; our home is mired in "the swamp of deceit." While Gina cries, Hialmar morosely observes that his "whole dream has vanished."

Beaming with satisfaction, Gregers confidently enters. Where he expected "the light of transfiguration" to shine from husband and wife, he is surprised to find nothing but "dullness, oppression, and gloom," he says. He cannot understand why Hialmar, with his sensitive perceptiveness, is unable to "feel a new consecration after the great crisis." Relling enters at this point, rudely asking Gregers his purpose in coming here. "To lay the foundations of a true marriage," responds young Werle. The physician reminds them that, although they are free to mess up their lives, they must remember a child is involved. Hedvig is at a critical age, he says, where she has "all sorts of mischief in her head." Hialmar promptly vows he shall protect his child "so long as I am above ground."

At this moment Mrs. Sorby pays them an unexpected visit. About to leave for the Höidal works where she and Werle are to be married, she wishes to say good-bye. Having been a friend of Mrs. Sorby for many years, Dr. Relling announces that he shall mourn his loss during a drinking binge with Molvik this night. Gregers threatens to let his father know of Mrs. Sorby's previous connection with Relling. He knows everything that can be truthfully said about me, answers the housekeeper, nor does he keep any secrets from me. Moreover, she tells Gregers, this marriage is not entirely one-sided; now that your father is going blind he needs someone like me "to stand beside him and care for him." Hialmar is startled. "Going blind?" he says wonderingly. "That's strange. He too going blind." Taking affectionate leave of Gina, Mrs. Sorby exits.

When Hedvig comes in, she shows her father a letter which Mrs. Sorby gave her as a birthday present. Written in Werle's hand, the letter grants a monthly allowance of one hundred crowns to Lieutenant Ekdal, which will, upon the old man's death, continue as a lifelong settlement upon Hedvig. Hilamar draws the shocking conclusion, and sends Hedvig out of the room. He turns to his wife, asking whether or not the child is really his daughter. Gina pleads ignorance and admits she does not know. "Gregers, I have no child!" wails Hialmar, while Hedvig rushes in and embraces her tearful father. He shrinks from her touch. "Keep far away. I cannot bear to see you," he cries. "Oh! Those eyes!" And Hialmar plunges out of the house. Gina tries to comfort her sobbing daughter. Going out to fetch Ekdal, she leaves Gregers and Hedvig alone onstage.

Young Werle suggests that Hedvig sacrifice the wild duck to show her love for her father. This free will offering of "the dearest treasure you have in the world" will provide Hialmar proof of Hedvig's devotion. The child is hopeful and says she will ask her grandfather to shoot the bird for her. Gina comes back, saying that Ekdal had gone out with Relling and Molvik. Gregers wonders that he should go out "this evening, when his mind so sorely needs to wrestle in solitude." The curtain falls as Gina tries to comfort the sobbing Hedvig.

Commentary

In this act, Gregers believes his mission is accomplished. Having disclosed the truth about Hialmar's family, the young Werle looks forward to viewing the process of purification in his friend. The outcome, however, is ironic: in a fit of self-indulgent martyrdom Hialmar rejects his family. Though he has said he will protect his child until he is buried, the father renounces Hedvig as soon as he discovers she is old Werle's daughter. Escaping from the inner conflict this knowledge has aroused, Hialmar goes off on a drinking binge with Relling and Volvik.

Gregers, however, still believes that his friend is capable of laying the foundations of a new life. He now carries his "claim of the ideal" to Hedvig. Gregers believes that if she would show her love by sacrificing the wild duck, Ekdal will recognize the value of his family ties. He furthermore thinks that once the wild duck is destroyed, the Ekdal household will be freed from the curse of delusion and fantasy. By this train of thought Gregers unwittingly commits the same logical error he tries to make Hialmar avoid: he acts on the belief that if the symbol of fantasy is effaced, then the Ekdals' lives will be devoted to a truthful acceptance of their lot.

ACT V

Summary

Cold, gray morning light illuminates the stage, and Hialmar has not returned. Dr. Relling informs them he is asleep on the sofa in his apartment. "How can he sleep?" asks the despairing Hedvig, and Gregers answers that the man needs rest after "the spiritual conflict which has rent him." Relling differs, observing that he noticed no such tumult in Hialmar. When Gina and Hedvig are out of the room, Gregers says he is amazed that Relling cannot see the greatness of Hialmar Ekdal's character. Raised by hysterical maiden aunts, replies the physician, Hialmar only passed as a great man. His father "who has been an ass all his days" approved of everything the young man did. The doctor continues:

> But then when our dear sweet Hialmar went to college he at once passed for the great light of the future amongst his comrades too! He was handsome, the rascal — red and white — a shopgirl's dream of manly beauty; and with his superficially emotional temperament and his sympathetic voice for declaiming other people's verses and other people's thoughts — [Here Gregers interrupts angrily.]

The physician begins to diagnose young Werle. "You, who are always in a delirium of hero worship," are sick. You must always have something outside yourself to adore, and Gregers admits the truth of Relling's observations. Relling tells young Werle that in Hialmar's case of sickness he applies the "usual remedy": "I am cultivating the life illusion in him," says the physician. As for Molvik, "since the harmless creature would have succumbed to self-contempt and despair" long ago, Relling, by way of cure, invented his being "demonic." Old Ekdal has found his own remedy, for "there is not a happier sportsman in the world than that old man pottering about" in the garret. Gregers agrees that the unfortunate old man has "indeed had to narrow the ideals of his youth." Don't use that foreign word "ideals," Relling retorts. "We have the excellent native word: lies." Gregers vows to rest only after he has freed Hialmar from the doctor's clutches. "Rob the average man of his life illusion and you rob him of his happiness at the same stroke," warns Relling before he goes. With a final word to Hedvig to remind her that the "fearless spirit of sacrifice" would recall her father, Gregers also exits.

"How would you go about shooting a duck, grandfather?" the child asks as Lieutenant Ekdal emerges from the garret. In the breast, against the feathers, he answers, and retires into his room. Hedvig gingerly takes the double-barrelled pistol from the shelf, hastily replacing it when Gina enters. Her mother bids her prepare a breakfast tray for father; suddenly Hialmar appears, bleary-eyed and dishevelled. The child cries out for joy, but he turns away, telling Gina, "Keep her away from me, I say." Hedvig disappears without a word.

Hialmar asks his wife to pack his clothes for he intends to leave and "my helpless father will come with me." Searching for his papers in Hedvig's room, he cruelly orders her out. In my last moments in this my former home, Ekdal tells Gina, "I wish to be spared from interlopers." Hedvig stands alone onstage, fighting back her tears. Thinking of the wild duck, she takes the pistol and softly steals into the garret.

Meanwhile Hialmar, complaining about "the exhausting preparations" for leaving, sits down to his coffee, munching on heavily buttered bread. As Gina points out how difficult it will be to find accommodations for the birds and pigeons which his father needs, Hialmar decides to stay at home for a day or so until an available apartment turns up. He also decides to save the letter from Werle; he says it really belongs to father and he had no right to tear it up. Gregers enters at this point to find Hialmar gluing the torn pieces of paper together. He is disappointed to find Ekdal ready to leave the house and reminds him of the invention he must finish. There is no invention, answers Hialmar bitterly; it was all Relling's idea, and he continued to think of it because it made Hedvig so happy. "How unutterably I loved the child," moans the father, and now I begin to doubt that perhaps she has never honestly loved me. Hearing the duck quacking in the garret, Hialmar believes his father is hunting in there, but Gregar's face shows joy as he says that Hialmar may yet have proof of Hedvig's love. Continuing his dark thoughts, Ekdal asserts that, since she faces a rich future, the wealth will turn her head and Hedvig will surely leave him:

> If I then asked her [he goes on], 'Hedvig, are you willing to renounce that life for me?' ...you would soon hear what answer I should get.

A pistol shot rings out from the garret. Gina rushes in, worried that the old man is shooting by himself. Excitedly Gregers explains that Hedvig had her grandfather shoot the bird for if she sacrificed her most cherished possession "then you would surely come to love her again." When old Ekdal looks out from his room, they have a sudden foreboding, and rush into the garret. Hialmar and Gregers carry Hedvig to the sofa, and Relling, having come when called, pronounces her dead. Gina sobs and reaches for her husband. "We must help each other to bear it, for now she belongs to us both," she says.

Relling gazes searchingly at Gregers; the death was no accident, he declares accusingly. "Hedvig has not died in vain," young Werle asserts. "Did you not see how sorrow set free what was noble in Hialmar?" That is only temporary, answers the doctor. Within a year, Hedvig "will be nothing to him but a pretty theme for declamation." Hialmar shall soon steep himself in a "syrup of sentiment and self-admiration and self-pity," Relling tells the shocked Gregers. If you are right, then life is not worth living, the young man tells him:

Life would be quite tolerable after all [says the physician] if only we could get rid of the confounded duns that keep pestering us in our poverty with the claims of the ideal.

In that case, says Gregers as he prepares to go, I am glad for my destiny—"to be thirteenth at table." "The devil it is," mutters Relling as the curtain rings down.

Commentary
Life would be quite tolerable, Relling says as he expresses the keynote of the play, if imperfect souls do not destroy themselves by trying to meet the claims of the ideal. Unable to accept this doctrine as an acceptable standard of life, Gregers chooses to be "thirteenth at table"—to remain outside the circle of the normal human condition. Hialmar, on the other hand, lacking personal integrity, will survive because he can easily build up a new series of self-deceptions to overcome temporary disillusion. He and Gina will continue their life together, sustaining their sense of personal worth with fresh fantasies.

GENERAL ANALYSIS

The Wild Duck represents an investigation of a problem that Ibsen wrestled with throughout his life. Always concerned with "the claim of the ideal" and proselytizing this claim to others, Ibsen, on the other hand, found in himself qualities of material indulgence and a weakness for worldly recognition. He suspected that he himself, like Gregers, substituted a missionary zeal to reform others for a failure to actively fight for the reforms he desired.

Thus *The Wild Duck* represents a personal compromise for Ibsen. From the problems of self-fulfillment he considered in *A Doll's House* and *Ghosts,* to the cult of the lone strong-willed individual in *Enemy of the People* (produced two years before *The Wild Duck*), Ibsen confronted the logical outcome of a situation where an idealist carries his message as an intrusion on the normal world of mediocrity and hollowness of soul. *The Wild Duck,* in a sense, solved Ibsen's own moral dilemma as he struggled between a militant idealism (as in *Brand* and *Enemy of the People*) and his own worldly temperament. With a pragmatic, anti-romantic viewpoint, this drama presents a continuum between the opposing values of the Ideal and the Real.

By including many symbols in the play that refer to his personal memories, Ibsen provides further evidence that proves *The Wild Duck* is an outcome of his personal struggles. Hedvig, who stands between Gregers' idealism and Hialmar's romantic self-deceptions, is the name of Ibsen's favorite sister. Providing Ibsen with his only family contact, she was deeply religious and tried to imbue her brother with her mystic beliefs. Hedvig, who tells Gregers she reads from an old picture book called *The History of London,* represents Ibsen's mysticism. As a small child he too was fascinated by this same book mentioned in the play, whose illustrations of castles and churches and sailboats bore his thoughts to romantic far off places. Hedvig says the book was left by an old sea captain whom they call "the Flying Dutchman," and this too is true of the book Ibsen had as a child. The "captain," a native of the town of Risör, had been first enslaved in the Barbary states and then imprisoned in England. He died the year Ibsen was born, and the author invested all his romantic dreams in this unknown tragic figure.

STRUCTURE, TECHNIQUE, AND THEME

The Wild Duck's thematic duality—reality versus idealism—becomes a structural feature of the play. Each scene illustrates this dualism. First Gregers confronts his father, a realist, and accuses him of a life built on lies and deception. In the following scene, Gregers confronts Hialmar and begins to rescue his friend from a life of self-delusion. Act III represents the antagonism between the realist Relling and young Werle, while Act IV exposes the paradox between Gregers' principles and the impossibility of realizing them. In the final scene, the duality becomes rationalized with Hedvig's suicide indicating the failure of applying pure principles to inappropriate situations. In effect, Ibsen concludes that life is a dynamic process whose only truth is based on any system which supports an individual's will to survive; life cannot exist according to principle but according to a compromise between emotional needs and the environment.

The central symbol of the play—an image borrowed from romanticism—further illustrates this duality. Ironically Ibsen uses it to destroy the very romanticism he describes in his characters. In a little poem called "The Sea Bird," written by Welhaven, one of Norway's most famous romantic poets, a wild duck dies from the shot of a careless hunter and dives silently to the bottom of the sea. Halvdan Koht, an Ibsen biographer, expresses one aspect of the double-viewed meaning of the symbol:

> The broken-winged duck [he writes] which gathered around it the dreams in the Ekdal home sent a strange tremulous flute note into the harsh, cold realism which otherwise gave such a sinister air to the play.

The "sinister air" Koht refers to is the resolution between the shabby, unromantic atmosphere of Ekdal's household and Hialmar's fantasy life expressed by the wilderness hunting ground in the garret, the hopes of Hedvig and their realization, and Ekdal's imitative life-values with his imaginary invention.

Ibsen furthermore expresses the paradoxical nature of life with his use of humor. Although the Ekdal household is a tragic one, eventually sacrificing Hedvig to Hialmar's personal emptiness, the comedy of the situation is unmistakable and serves to heighten the seriousness of Ibsen's theme. Hialmar's affections, his poses, his ridiculous interest in richly buttered bread and cold beer are not in themselves funny; these qualities underscore the pathetic mediocrity of his character. Gregers Werle, as well, ascetic and grimly serious about his "life's mission," is ridiculous when he proves his worldly ineptness by smoking up his room from a badly-fired stove, then flooding the floor to douse the fire. Molvik, the romantic clergyman who saves face by considering himself "demonic" is a funny character. Again this humorous quality serves a serious purpose. With Molvik, Ibsen ironically subverts the efficacy of Relling's romantic remedies of the "life-lies": at the side of Hedvig's corpse, Molvik's inappropriate declamation, "the child is not dead but sleepeth," underscores the pathetic futility of trying to avoid, by various methods, the tragic consequences of human frailty.

Using humor as a technique to indicate the tragic paradox between living according to principles of reality or ideality, and using dialogue and situations to underline the duality, Ibsen's *The Wild Duck* shows that life-truths are dynamic processes which sustain individuals according to their human weaknesses. According to this system, "life-lies" are life-truths, an idealistic point of view leads to self-deception, and "truth" is whatever belief an individual requires to sustain life.

CHARACTERS AND SYMBOLS

As in all of Ibsen's plays, the characters in *The Wild Duck* reflect each other and by mutual comparison amplify the dramatic theme and hasten events to their conclusion. In this play, however, the characters are not only related among themselves; they each bear relation to the integral symbolism of the play, especially the image of the wild duck. Only old Werle and Mrs. Sorby are excepted. Facing realities in their past and present, these pragmatic individuals successfully begin to build a life based on mutual trust and truthfulness. Werle, in fact, desired that his servant get rid of the wounded bird: he has no need of a wild duck.

Hedvig, the innocent victim of the tension between the two men who stand for the "lie" and the "truth" has much in common with the wild duck. Too inexperienced to recognize the shallow affection Hialmar accords her, she is happy at home, for, like the wild duck who has forgotten the freedom of sky, sea, and woods in captivity, she has had no contrasting experience in life to provide her with perspective on those she lives with. Moreover, since she is Gina's natural daughter, she, like the wounded bird, is an indirect present from old Werle to the Ekdals. When Hedvig realizes that her father rejects her, she plans to sacrifice the wild duck to show her love and recall his. This is her attempt to adjust to the new truth Gregers has revealed. Finding her free will offering insufficient, however, Hedvig goes one step further and kills herself. With this suicide, the wild duck and Hedvig become joined: she dies in lieu of the bird as if to prove Gregers' warning that the wild duck, after once glimpsing the blue sky, will pine for her former freedom. Hedvig, with a glimpse of the truth of her father's feelings for her, dies because she cannot bear to live with the knowledge of her origins.

Gregers Werle, appearing as a bird of ill omen, tries to rescue the Ekdals from the swamp of their self-deception. He thinks Hialmar a wounded bird who will drown in the depths of the sea unless Gregers, like his father's "amazingly clever dog," will dive to retrieve him. However, he soon discovers his own self-deception. Encountering failure at proclaiming the truth, discovering his admired friend Hialmar to be a hollow-souled egotist, Gregers recognizes that lies are necessary to existence. Unwilling, however, to accept this pragmatic solution to life, Gregers himself becomes like the wild duck, who, when wounded, bites fast to the underwater seaweed and drowns: despite the ruined dreams, he still clings to the illusory "claim of the ideal." Despairing to find a worthwhile way of life, he dooms himself to be "thirteenth at table" — an uncompromising tenacity to principle which can only end in suicide.

Where Gregers proves to be an unsuccessful retriever, Dr. Relling is successful. Like Werle's "amazingly clever dog" the physician rescues individuals from the "marsh poisons" of their unfulfilled desires. By providing these wounded "wild ducks" with a new environment in their imaginations, he encourages his friends to adjust to the unsatisfactory circumstances of life. His romanticism thus generates the very force for men of weak character to maintain their hold on reality.

Another significant symbolic idea in *The Wild Duck* is that of photography. That Hialmar Ekdal is a photographer underscores the imitative nature of his way of life. Taking ideas and ideals from other sources, Hialmar presents an image of nobility and an appearance of character depth he does not really possess. In the course of the play, Hialmar is busy at retouching — we never see him take any pictures. By the same token, Ekdal retouches his own self-image, minimizing his character blemishes until his whole life is a distortion of the truth.

CHARACTER ANALYSIS

Gregers Werle

Gregers Werle is the son of a man he detests and he has avoided his father by spending the past fifteen years in the family mining concern, the Höidal works, in the northern forests of Norway. In the course of the play Ibsen establishes that, because he is so unattractive in appearance, Gregers has abandoned the hope of settling down with his own family; his long brooding solitude has prevented him, furthermore, from understanding his father. Young Werle, an idealist, feels that his mission is to Advocate & Preach Truth and Purity of Soul whenever he can. In the events of *The Wild Duck,* Gregers plays a major role of proving to others the virtues of the "claim of the ideal."

Hakon Werle

The old man himself, Hakon Werle, has allegedly driven his sick wife to her death by carrying on love affairs in his own home. First he caused his young serving girl, Gina, to become pregnant. Arranging her marriage with Hialmar Ekdal, the son of his former partner, Werle also provided money for the young man to take up the profession of photography. Hialmar is pleased with his marriage and believes that Gina's child is his own daughter, now fourteen years old. At present, Werle lives with his housekeeper, Mrs. Sorby, and intends to marry her. Both have no secrets about their past life and have exposed to each other all their previous connections.

Lieutenant Ekdal

Werle's former partner is now a broken old man. He does odd jobs of copy work for Werle's bookkeeper which provides him with enough means to buy an occasional bottle of cognac. Fourteen years ago, when old Ekdal was active at the Höidal works, the company appropriated a large quantity of lumber from government-owned land. Ekdal paid for this crime by serving a jail sentence and losing his reputation. He now lives with Hialmar and Gina.

The other characters bear brief mention. *Dr. Relling*, the realist of the play, lives in a downstairs apartment from the Ekdals. His roommate is *Molvik*, a weak-charactered clergyman. *Hedvig*, Ekdal's adolescent daughter, is the sensitive innocent who suffers the most in this drama of misapplied idealism.

DRAMA OF IBSEN

Although the plays are interesting for their social message, Ibsenite drama would not survive today were it not for his consummate skill as a technician. Each drama is carefully wrought into a tight logical construction where characters are clearly delineated and interrelated, and where events have a symbolic as well as actual significance. The symbolism in Ibsen's plays is rarely overworked. Carefully integrated to unify the setting, events, and character portrayals, the symbols are incidental and subordinate to the truth and consistency of his picture of life.

Having been interested in studying painting as a youth, Ibsen was always conscious of making accurate observations. As a dramatist, he considered himself a photographer as well, using his powers of observation as a lens, while his finished plays represented the proofs of a skilled darkroom technician. The realism of his plays, the credibility of his characters, the immediacy of his themes attest to these photographic skills at which Ibsen so consciously worked. Among his countless revisions for each drama, he paid special heed to the accuracy of his dialogue. Through constant rewriting, he brought out the maximum meaning in the fewest words, attempting to fit each speech into the character of the speaker. In addition, Ibsen's ability as a poet contributed a special beauty to his terse prose.

The problems of Ibsen's social dramas are consistent throughout all his works. George Brandes, a contemporary critic, said of Ibsen, as early as the 1860s, that "his progress from one work to the other is not due to a rich variety of themes and ideas, but on the contrary to a perpetual scrutiny of the same general questions, regarded from different points of view." In *A Doll's House,* he especially probed the problems of the social passivity assigned to women in a male-oriented society. After considering the plight of Nora Helmer, he then investigated what would happen had she remained at home. The consequence of his thoughts appears as *Ghosts.* Going one step further, Ibsen investigated the fallacies inherent in his own idealism. Much as Pastor Manders applies empty principles to actual situations Gregers Werle is shown trying to impose an idealistic viewpoint when circumstances demand that individuals can only accept their lives by clinging to "life-lies." Although *The Wild Duck* differs in treatment from *Hedda Gabler,* the plays both have protagonists who find in their imaginations an outlet for their frustrations. *Hedda Gabler,* however, with its emphasis on individual psychology, is a close scrutiny of a woman like Nora Helmer or Mrs. Alving who searches for personal meaning in a society which denies freedom of expression.

Professor Koht, a renown scholar, sums up the dramatist's investigations:

> The thing which filled [Ibsen's] mind was the individual man, and he measured the worth of a community according as it helped or hindered a man in being himself. He had an ideal standard which he placed upon the community and it was from this measuring that his social criticism proceeded.

Secondary to, and in connection with, his idea that the individual is of supreme importance, Ibsen believed that the final personal tragedy comes from a denial of love. From this viewpoint we see that Torvald is an incomplete individual because he attaches more importance to a crime against society than a sin against love. The same is true for Pastor Manders. Hedda Gabler is doomed to a dissatisfied life because she too is unable to love, and Hedvig's tragic suicide is the result of her pathetic attempt to recall her father's affections. In Ibsen's other plays, particularly *Brand,* this theme is of primary importance.

In an age when nations were striving for independence, Ibsen's sense of democracy was politically prophetic. He believed, not that "right" was the preogative of the mass majority, but that it resided among the educated minority. In the development and enrichment of the individual, he saw the only hope of a really cultured and enlightened society.

IBSEN'S CONTRIBUTIONS TO THE THEATER

Until the latter part of the nineteenth century, theater remained a vehicle of entertainment. Insights into the human condition were merely incidental factors in the dramatist's art. Ibsen, however, contributed a new significance to drama which changed the development of modern theater. Discovering dramatic material in everyday situations was the beginning of a realism that novelists as different as Zola and Flaubert were already exploiting. When Nora quietly confronts her husband with "Sit down, Torvald, you and I have much to say to each other," drama became no longer a mere diversion, but an experience closely impinging on the lives of the playgoers themselves. With Ibsen, the stage became a pulpit, while the dramatist exhorting his audience to reassess the values of society, became the minister of a new social responsibility.

COMPLETE LIST OF IBSEN'S DRAMAS

VERSE 1850 Catiline
1850 The Warrior's Barrow
1853 St. John's Night
1855 Lady Inger of Ostratt
1856 The Feast of Solhaug
1857 Olaf Liljekrans
1858 The Vikings of Helgeland

    1862 Love's Comedy
    1864 The Pretenders
    1866 Brand
    1867 Peer Gynt
    1873 Emperor and Galilean (blank verse)

PROSE 1869 The League of Youth
    1877 The Pillars of Society
    1879 A Doll's House
    1881 Ghosts
    1882 An Enemy of the People
    1884 The Wild Duck
    1886 Rosmersholm
    1888 The Lady from the Sea
    1890 Hedda Gabler
    1892 The Master Builder
    1894 Little Eyolf
    1896 John Gabriel Borkman
    1900 When We Dead Awaken

SELECTED BIBLIOGRAPHY

Brian W. Downs, *A Study of Six Plays by Ibsen;* Cambridge, England: 1950.

Edmund Gosse, *Henrik Ibsen;* London: 1907.

Halvdan Koht, *The Life of Ibsen,* translated by R. L. McMahon and H. A. Larsen; 2 vols.; New York: 1931.

Janko Lavrin, *Ibsen, An Approach;* London: 1950.

M. S. Moses, *Henrik Ibsen, the Man and His Plays;* Boston: 1920.

George Bernard Shaw, *The Quintessence of Ibsenism;* Ayot St. Lawrence edition, vol. 19; London: 1921.

Hermann J. Wiegand, *The Modern Ibsen;* New York: 1925.

Adolph Edouard Zucker, *Ibsen, the Master Builder;* New York: 1929.

QUESTIONS FOR DISCUSSION

1. Using specific examples, discuss how Ibsen's "progress from one work to the other" is due to "a perpetual scrutiny of the same general questions regarded from different points of view."

2. Do you feel that Ibsen's drama is "dated"? To defend your view, cite dramatic themes in these plays which you consider to be universal, or limited in scope.

3. Often considered grim and oppressive, Ibsen's social dramas always contain considerable humor. From your own reading of these three plays, discuss the scenes which a comedy-conscious stage manager would be most likely to exploit for humor.

4. At least one character in each of these plays prefers his imaginary view of life to a realistic viewpoint. With this in mind, discuss the life-views of Pastor Manders, Hialmar Ekdal, and Dr. Stockmann.

5. What additional insight into the following characters does their choice of vocation provide: Hialmar Ekdal—photographer; Oswald Alving—painter; Dr. Stockmann—medical doctor?

6. For each of the three plays, show how the first act forewarns the audience of almost all the forthcoming events in the rest of the drama.

7. Point out some instances where Ibsen is able to "externalize" inner problems by using effective symbols. (Example: Oswald's physical disease which stands for a morally diseased society.)

8. What are the "ghosts" in *Ghosts?* Discuss some "ghosts" of contemporary society to which we, as individuals or as a nation, still succumb.

9. In your own words, explain why Dr. Relling prefers "the excellent native word — lies" to the word "ideals."

10. Discuss the relationship *The Wild Duck* bears to Ibsen's dramatic development.

11. Explain the symbolic significance of hereditary disease in *Ghosts*.

NOTES

NOTES

NOTES

NOTES

NOTES

NOTES

This is the TITLE INDEX, indexing the over 200 titles available by Series, by Library and by Volume Number for both the BASIC LIBRARY SERIES and the AUTHORS LIBRARY SERIES.

TITLE	SERIES	LIBRARY	Vol
Absalom, Absalom!	Basic	American Lit	4
	Authors	Faulkner	3
Adonais (in <u>Keats & Shelley</u>)	Basic	English Lit	1
Aeneid, The	Basic	Classics	1
Aeschylus' Oresteia (in <u>Agamemnon</u>)	Basic	Classics	1
Agamemnon	Basic	Classics	1
Alice in Wonderland	Basic	English Lit	3
All That Fall (in <u>Waiting for Godot</u>)	Basic	European Lit	1
All the King's Men	Basic	American Lit	6
All Quiet on the Western Front	Basic	European Lit	2
All's Well That Ends Well	Basic	Shakespeare	1
	Authors	Shakespeare	8
American, The	Basic	American Lit	2
	Authors	James	6
American Tragedy, An	Basic	American Lit	3
Animal Farm	Basic	English Lit	5
Anna Karenina	Basic	European Lit	3
Antigone (in <u>Oedipus Trilogy</u>)	Basic	Classics	1
Antony and Cleopatra	Basic	Shakespeare	2
	Authors	Shakespeare	9
Apology (in <u>Plato's Euthyphro....</u>)	Basic	Classics	1
Aristotle's Ethics	Basic	Classics	1
Arms and the Man (in <u>Shaw's Pygmalion....</u>)	Basic	English Lit	6
	Authors	Shaw	11
"Artificial Nigger, The" (in <u>O'Connor's Short Stories</u>)	Basic	American Lit	7
As I Lay Dying	Basic	American Lit	4
	Authors	Faulkner	3
Assistant, The	Basic	American Lit	6
As You Like It	Basic	Shakespeare	1
	Authors	Shakespeare	8
Autobiography of Benjamin Franklin	Basic	American Lit	1
Autobiography of Malcolm X, The	Basic	American Lit	6
Awakening, The	Basic	American Lit	2
Babbitt	Basic	American Lit	3
	Authors	Lewis	7
"Bear, The" (in <u>Go Down, Moses</u>)	Basic	American Lit	4
	Authors	Faulkner	3
Bear, The	Basic	American Lit	4
	Authors	Faulkner	3
Bell Jar, The	Basic	American Lit	6
Beowulf	Basic	Classics	3
Billy Budd	Basic	American Lit	1
Birds, The (in <u>Lysistrata....</u>)	Basic	Classics	1
Black Boy	Basic	American Lit	4

TITLE	SERIES	LIBRARY	Vol
Black Like Me	Basic	American Lit	6
Bleak House	Basic	English Lit	3
	Authors	Dickens	1
Bourgeois Gentleman, The (in Tartuffe....)	Basic	European Lit	1
Brave New World	Basic	English Lit	5
Brave New World Revisited (in Brave New World)	Basic	English Lit	5
Brothers Karamozov, The	Basic	European Lit	3
	Authors	Dostoevsky	2
Caesar and Cleopatra (in Shaw's Man and Superman....)	Basic	English Lit	6
	Authors	Shaw	11
Call of the Wild, The	Basic	American Lit	3
Candide	Basic	European Lit	1
Canterbury Tales, The	Basic	Classics	3
"Cask of Amontillado, The" (in Poe's Short Stories)	Basic	American Lit	1
Catch-22	Basic	American Lit	6
Catcher in the Rye, The	Basic	American Lit	6
Choephori (in Agamemnon)	Basic	Classics	1
Clouds, The (in Lysistrata....)	Basic	Classics	1
Color Purple, The	Basic	American Lit	6
Comedy of Errors, The	Basic	Shakespeare	1
	Authors	Shakespeare	8
Connecticut Yankee in King Arthur's Court, A	Basic	American Lit	2
	Authors	Twain	13
Count of Monte Cristo, The	Basic	European Lit	1
Crime and Punishment	Basic	European Lit	3
	Authors	Dostoevsky	2
Crito (in Plato's Euthyphro....)	Basic	Classics	1
Crucible, The	Basic	American Lit	6
Cry, the Beloved Country	Basic	English Lit	5
Cyrano de Bergerac	Basic	European Lit	1
Daisy Miller	Basic	American Lit	2
	Authors	James	6
David Copperfield	Basic	English Lit	3
	Authors	Dickens	1
Day of the Locust, The (in Miss Lonelyhearts....)	Basic	American Lit	5
Death of a Salesman	Basic	American Lit	6
Deerslayer, The	Basic	American Lit	1
"Delta Autumn" (in Go Down, Moses)	Basic	American Lit	4
Demian	Basic	European Lit	2
Diary of Anne Frank, The	Basic	European Lit	2
"Displaced Person, The" (in O'Connor's Short Stories)	Basic	American Lit	7
Divine Comedy I: Inferno	Basic	Classics	3
Divine Comedy II: Purgatorio	Basic	Classics	3
Divine Comedy III: Paradiso	Basic	Classics	3
Doctor Faustus	Basic	Classics	3
Doll's House, A (in Ibsen's Plays I)	Basic	European Lit	4
Don Quixote	Basic	Classics	3
Dr. Jekyll and Mr. Hyde	Basic	English Lit	3

TITLE	SERIES	LIBRARY	Vol
Dracula	Basic	English Lit	3
Dune	Basic	American Lit	6
Electra (in Euripides' Electra & Medea)	Basic	Classics	1
Emerson's Essays	Basic	American Lit	1
Emily Dickinson: Selected Poems	Basic	American Lit	2
Emma	Basic	English Lit	1
Endgame (in Waiting for Godot)	Basic	European Lit	1
Enemy of the People, An (in Ibsen's Plays II)	Basic	European Lit	4
Ethan Frome	Basic	American Lit	3
Eumenides (in Agamemnon)	Basic	Classics	1
Euripides' Electra	Basic	Classics	1
Euripides' Medea	Basic	Classics	1
Euthyphro (in Plato's Euthyphro....)	Basic	Classics	1
Eve of St. Agnes, The (in Keats & Shelley)	Basic	English Lit	1
"Everything That Rises Must Converge" (in O'Connor's Short Stories)	Basic	American Lit	7
Faerie Queene, The	Basic	Classics	4
"Fall of the House of Usher, The" (in Poe's Short Stories)	Basic	American Lit	1
Far from the Madding Crowd	Basic	English Lit	3
	Authors	Hardy	4
Farewell to Arms, A	Basic	American Lit	4
	Authors	Hemingway	5
Fathers and Sons	Basic	European Lit	3
Faust, Pt. I and Pt. II	Basic	European Lit	2
"Fire and the Hearth, The" (in Go Down, Moses)	Basic	American Lit	4
Flies, The (in No Exit & The Flies)	Basic	European Lit	1
For Whom the Bell Tolls	Basic	American Lit	4
	Authors	Hemingway	5
"Four Quartets, The" (in T.S. Eliot's Major Poems and Plays)	Basic	English Lit	6
Frankenstein	Basic	English Lit	1
French Lieutenant's Woman, The	Basic	English Lit	5
Frogs, The (in Lysistrata....)	Basic	Classics	1
Ghosts (in Ibsen's Plays II)	Basic	European Lit	4
Giants in the Earth	Basic	European Lit	4
Glass Menagerie, The	Basic	American Lit	6
Go Down, Moses	Basic	American Lit	4
	Authors	Faulkner	3
Good Country People (in O'Connor's Short Stories)	Basic	American Lit	7
Good Earth, The	Basic	American Lit	4
Good Man is Hard to Find, A (in O'Connor's Short Stories)	Basic	American Lit	7
Grapes of Wrath, The	Basic	American Lit	4
	Authors	Steinbeck	12
Great Expectations	Basic	English Lit	3
	Authors	Dickens	1
Great Gatsby, The	Basic	American Lit	4
Greek Classics	Basic	Classics	2
Gulliver's Travels	Basic	English Lit	1

TITLE	SERIES	LIBRARY	Vol
Hamlet	Basic	Shakespeare	2
	Authors	Shakespeare	9
Hard Times	Basic	English Lit	3
	Authors	Dickens	1
Heart of Darkness	Basic	English Lit	5
Hedda Gabler (in Ibsen's Plays I)	Basic	European Lit	4
Henry IV, Part 1	Basic	Shakespeare	3
	Authors	Shakespeare	10
Henry IV, Part 2	Basic	Shakespeare	3
	Authors	Shakespeare	10
Henry V	Basic	Shakespeare	3
	Authors	Shakespeare	10
Henry VI, Pts. 1,2, & 3	Basic	Shakespeare	3
	Authors	Shakespeare	10
Hobbit, The (in The Lord of the Rings)	Basic	English Lit	5
House of the Seven Gables, The	Basic	American Lit	1
Huckleberry Finn	Basic	American Lit	2
	Authors	Twain	13
"A Hunger Artist" (in Kafka's Short Stories)	Basic	European Lit	2
Ibsen's Plays I	Basic	European Lit	4
Ibsen's Plays II	Basic	European Lit	4
Iliad, The	Basic	Classics	1
Invisible Man, The	Basic	American Lit	7
Ivanhoe	Basic	English Lit	1
Jane Eyre	Basic	English Lit	3
Joseph Andrews	Basic	English Lit	1
Jude the Obscure	Basic	English Lit	3
	Authors	Hardy	4
Julius Caesar	Basic	Shakespeare	2
	Authors	Shakespeare	9
Jungle, The	Basic	American Lit	3
Kafka's Short Stories	Basic	European Lit	2
Keats & Shelley	Basic	English Lit	1
Kidnapped (in Treasure Island & Kidnapped)	Basic	English Lit	4
King Lear	Basic	Shakespeare	2
	Authors	Shakespeare	9
King Oedipus (in The Oedipus Trilogy)	Basic	Classics	1
Krapp's Last Tape (in Waiting for Godot)	Basic	European Lit	1
Last of the Mohicans, The	Basic	American Lit	1
Le Morte d'Arthur	Basic	Classics	4
Leaves of Grass	Basic	American Lit	1
Les Miserables	Basic	European Lit	1
"The Life You Save May Be Your Own" in O'Connor's Short Stories)	Basic	American Lit	7
Light in August	Basic	American Lit	4
	Authors	Faulkner	3
Lord Jim	Basic	English Lit	5
Lord of the Flies	Basic	English Lit	5
Lord of the Rings, The	Basic	English Lit	5

TITLE	SERIES	LIBRARY	Vol
Lost Horizon	Basic	English Lit	5
"Love Song of J. Alfred Prufrock, The" (in T.S. Eliot's Major Poems and Plays)	Basic	English Lit	6
Love's Labour's Lost (in Comedy of Errors....)	Basic	Shakespeare	1
	Authors	Shakespeare	8
Lysistrata & Other Comedies	Basic	Classics	1
Macbeth	Basic	Shakespeare	2
	Authors	Shakespeare	9
Madame Bovary	Basic	European Lit	1
Main Street	Basic	American Lit	3
	Authors	Lewis	7
Man and Superman (in Shaw's Man and Superman)	Basic	English Lit	6
	Authors	Shaw	11
Manchild in the Promised Land	Basic	American Lit	7
Mayor of Casterbridge, The	Basic	English Lit	3
	Authors	Hardy	4
Measure for Measure	Basic	Shakespeare	1
	Authors	Shakespeare	8
Medea (in Euripides' Electra & Medea)	Basic	Classics	1
Merchant of Venice, The	Basic	Shakespeare	1
	Authors	Shakespeare	8
Merry Wives of Windsor, The (in All's Well....)	Basic	Shakespeare	1
	Authors	Shakespeare	8
"Metamorphosis, The" (in Kafka's Short Stories)	Basic	European Lit	2
Middlemarch	Basic	English Lit	4
Midsummer Night's Dream, A	Basic	Shakespeare	1
	Authors	Shakespeare	8
Mill on the Floss, The	Basic	The English Lit	4
Misanthrope (in Tartuffe....)	Basic	European Lit	1
Miss Lonelyhearts	Basic	American Lit	5
Moby Dick	Basic	American Lit	1
Moll Flanders	Basic	English Lit	1
Mother Night (in Vonnegut's Major Works)	Basic	American Lit	7
Mrs. Dalloway	Basic	English Lit	5
Much Ado About Nothing	Basic	Shakespeare	1
	Authors	Shakespeare	8
"Murder in the Cathedral" (in T.S. Eliot's Major Poems and Plays)	Basic	English Lit	6
My Antonia	Basic	American Lit	3
Mythology	Basic	Classics	1
Native Son	Basic	American Lit	5
New Testament	Basic	Classics	4
Nichomachean Ethics (in Aristotle's Ethics)	Basic	Classics	1
Nineteen Eighty-Four	Basic	English Lit	6
No Exit	Basic	European Lit	1
Notes from the Underground	Basic	European Lit	3
	Authors	Dostoevsky	2
O'Connor's Short Stories	Basic	American Lit	7
Odyssey, The	Basic	Classics	1

TITLE	SERIES	LIBRARY	Vol
Oedipus at Colonus (in The Oedipus Trilogy)	Basic	Classics	1
Oedipus the King (in The Oedipus Trilogy)	Basic	Classics	1
Oedipus Trilogy, The	Basic	Classics	1
Of Human Bondage	Basic	English Lit	6
Of Mice and Men	Basic	American Lit	5
	Authors	Steinbeck	12
Old Man and the Sea, The	Basic	American Lit	7
	Authors	Hemingway	5
"Old People, The" (in Go Down, Moses)	Basic	American Lit	4
Old Testament	Basic	Classics	4
Oliver Twist	Basic	English Lit	4
	Authors	Dickens	1
One Day in the Life of Ivan Denisovich	Basic	European Lit	3
One Flew Over the Cuckoo's Nest	Basic	American Lit	7
One Hundred Years of Solitude	Basic	American Lit	6
"On First Looking Into Chapman's Homer" (in Keats & Shelley)	Basic	English Lit	1
Othello	Basic	Shakespeare	2
	Authors	Shakespeare	9
Our Town	Basic	American Lit	5
Ox-Bow Incident, The	Basic	American Lit	7
"Ozymandias" (in Keats & Shelley)	Basic	English Lit	1
"Pantaloon in Black" (in Go Down, Moses)	Basic	American Lit	4
Paradise Lost	Basic	English Lit	2
Passage to India, A	Basic	English Lit	6
Patience (in Sir Gawain and the Green Knight)	Basic	Classics	4
Pearl, The	Basic	American Lit	5
	Authors	Steinbeck	12
Pearl (in Sir Gawain and the Green Knight)	Basic	Classics	4
Phaedo (in Plato's Euthyphro....)	Basic	Classics	1
Pilgrim's Progress, The	Basic	English Lit	2
Plague, The	Basic	European Lit	1
Plato's Euthyphro, Apology, Crito & Phaedo	Basic	Classics	1
Plato's The Republic	Basic	Classics	1
Poe's Short Stories	Basic	American Lit	1
Portrait of the Artist as a Young Man, A	Basic	English Lit	6
Portrait of a Lady, The	Basic	American Lit	2
	Authors	James	6
Power and the Glory, The	Basic	English Lit	6
Prelude, The	Basic	English Lit	2
Pride and Prejudice	Basic	English Lit	2
Prince, The	Basic	Classics	4
Prince and the Pauper, The	Basic	American Lit	2
	Authors	Twain	13
Purity (in Sir Gawain and the Green Knight)	Basic	Classics	4
"Purloined Letter, The" (in Poe's Short Stories)	Basic	American Lit	1
Pygmalion (in Shaw's Pygmalion....)	Basic	English Lit	6
	Authors	Shaw	11

TITLE	SERIES	LIBRARY	Vol
Red and the Black, The	Basic	European Lit	1
Red Badge of Courage, The	Basic	American Lit	2
Red Pony, The	Basic	American Lit	5
	Authors	Steinbeck	12
Republic, The (in Plato's The Republic)	Basic	Classics	1
Return of the Native, The	Basic	English Lit	4
	Authors	Hardy	4
Richard II	Basic	Shakespeare	3
	Authors	Shakespeare	10
Richard III	Basic	Shakespeare	3
	Authors	Shakespeare	10
Robinson Crusoe	Basic	English Lit	2
Roman Classics	Basic	Classics	2
Romeo and Juliet	Basic	Shakespeare	2
	Authors	Shakespeare	9
Scarlet Letter, The	Basic	American Lit	1
Secret Sharer, The (in Heart of Darkness)	Basic	English Lit	5
Separate Peace, A	Basic	American Lit	7
Shakespeare's Sonnets	Basic	Shakespeare	3
	Authors	Shakespeare	10
Shane	Basic	American Lit	7
Shaw's Man and Superman & Caesar and Cleopatra	Basic	English Lit	6
Shaw's Pygmalion & Arms and the Man	Basic	English Lit	6
Shelley (in Keats and Shelley)	Basic	English Lit	1
Siddhartha (in Steppenwolf & Siddhartha)	Basic	European Lit	2
Silas Marner	Basic	English Lit	4
Sir Gawain and the Green Knight	Basic	Classics	4
Sister Carrie	Basic	American Lit	3
Slaughterhouse Five (in Vonnegut's Major Works)	Basic	American Lit	7
Sons and Lovers	Basic	English Lit	6
Sound and the Fury, The	Basic	American Lit	5
	Authors	Faulkner	3
Steppenwolf	Basic	European Lit	2
Stranger, The	Basic	European Lit	1
Streetcar Named Desire, A (in The Glass Menagerie....)	Basic	American Lit	6
Sun Also Rises, The	Basic	American Lit	5
	Authors	Hemingway	5
T.S. Eliot's Major Poems and Plays	Basic	English Lit	6
Tale of Two Cities, A	Basic	English Lit	4
	Authors	Dickens	1
Taming of the Shrew, The	Basic	Shakespeare	1
	Authors	Shakespeare	8
Tartuffe	Basic	European Lit	1
Tempest, The	Basic	Shakespeare	1
	Authors	Shakespeare	8
Tender is the Night	Basic	American Lit	5
Tess of the D'Urbervilles	Basic	English Lit	4
	Authors	Hardy	4

TITLE	SERIES	LIBRARY	Vol
Three Musketeers, The	Basic	European Lit	1
To Kill a Mockingbird	Basic	American Lit	7
Tom Jones	Basic	English Lit	2
Tom Sawyer	Basic	American Lit	2
	Authors	Twain	13
Treasure Island	Basic	English Lit	4
Trial, The	Basic	European Lit	2
Tristram Shandy	Basic	English Lit	2
Troilus and Cressida	Basic	Shakespeare	1
	Authors	Shakespeare	8
Turn of the Screw, The (in Daisy Miller....)	Basic	American Lit	2
	Authors	James	6
Twelfth Night	Basic	Shakespeare	1
	Authors	Shakespeare	8
Two Gentlemen of Verona, The (in Comedy of Errors...)	Basic	Shakespeare	1
	Authors	Shakespeare	8
Typee (in Billy Budd & Typee)	Basic	American Lit	1
Ulysses	Basic	English Lit	6
Uncle Tom's Cabin	Basic	American Lit	2
Unvanquished, The	Basic	American Lit	5
	Authors	Faulkner	3
Utopia	Basic	Classics	4
Vanity Fair	Basic	English Lit	4
Vonnegut's Major Works	Basic	American Lit	7
Waiting for Godot	Basic	European Lit	1
Walden	Basic	American Lit	1
Walden Two	Basic	American Lit	7
War and Peace	Basic	European Lit	3
"Was" (in Go Down, Moses)	Basic	American Lit	4
"Waste Land, The" (in T.S. Eliot's Major Poems and Plays)	Basic	English Lit	6
White Fang (in Call of the Wild & White Fang)	Basic	American Lit	3
Who's Afraid of Virginia Woolf?	Basic	American Lit	7
Wild Duck, The (in Ibsen's Plays II)	Basic	European Lit	4
Winesburg, Ohio	Basic	American Lit	3
Winter's Tale, The	Basic	Shakespeare	1
	Authors	Shakespeare	8
Wuthering Heights	Basic	English Lit	4

This is the AUTHOR INDEX, listing the over 200 titles available by author and indexing them by Series, by Library and by Volume Number for both the BASIC LIBRARY SERIES and the AUTHORS LIBRARY SERIES.

AUTHOR	TITLE(S)	SERIES	LIBRARY	Vol
Aeschylus	Agamemnon, The Choephori, & The Eumenides	Basic	Classics	1
Albee, Edward	Who's Afraid of Virginia Woolf?	Basic	American Lit	7
Anderson, Sherwood	Winesburg, Ohio	Basic	American Lit	3
Aristophanes	Lysistrata * The Birds * Clouds * The Frogs	Basic	Classics	1
Aristotle	Aristotle's Ethics	Basic	Classics	1
Austen, Jane	Emma	Basic	English Lit	1
	Pride and Prejudice	Basic	English Lit	2
Beckett, Samuel	Waiting for Godot	Basic	European Lit	1
Beowulf	Beowulf	Basic	Classics	3
Beyle, Henri	see Stendhal			
Bronte, Charlotte	Jane Eyre	Basic	English Lit	3
Bronte, Emily	Wuthering Heights	Basic	English Lit	4
Brown, Claude	Manchild in the Promised Land	Basic	American Lit	7
Buck, Pearl	The Good Earth	Basic	American Lit	4
Bunyan, John	The Pilgrim's Progress	Basic	English Lit	2
Camus, Albert	The Plague * The Stranger	Basic	European Lit	1
Carroll, Lewis	Alice in Wonderland	Basic	English Lit	3
Cather, Willa	My Antonia	Basic	American Lit	3
Cervantes, Miguel de	Don Quixote	Basic	Classics	3
Chaucer, Geoffrey	The Canterbury Tales	Basic	Classics	3
Chopin, Kate	The Awakening	Basic	American Lit	2
Clark, Walter	The Ox-Bow Incident	Basic	American Lit	7
Conrad, Joseph	Heart of Darkness & The Secret Sharer * Lord Jim	Basic	English Lit	5
Cooper, James F.	The Deerslayer * The Last of the Mohicans	Basic	American Lit	1
Crane, Stephen	The Red Badge of Courage	Basic	American Lit	2
Dante	Divine Comedy I: Inferno * Divine Comedy II: Purgatorio * Divine Comedy III: Paradiso	Basic	Classsics	3
Defoe, Daniel	Moll Flanders	Basic	English Lit	1
	Robinson Crusoe	Basic	English Lit	2
Dickens, Charles	Bleak House * David Copper-field * Great Expectations * Hard Times	Basic	English Lit	3
	Oliver Twist * A Tale of Two Cities	Basic	English Lit	4
	Bleak House * David Copper-field * Great Expectations * Hard Times * Oliver Twist * A Tale of Two Cities	Authors	Dickens	1

AUTHOR	TITLE(S)	SERIES	LIBRARY	Vol
Dickinson, Emily	Emily Dickinson: Selected Poems	Basic	American Lit	2
Dostoevsky, Feodor	The Brothers Karamazov * Crime and Punishment * Notes from the Underground	Basic	European Lit	3
	The Brothers Karamazov * Crime and Punishment * Notes from the Underground	Authors	Dostoevsky	2
Dreiser, Theodore	An American Tragedy * Sister Carrie	Basic	American Lit	3
Dumas, Alexandre	The Count of Monte Cristo * The Three Musketeers	Basic	European Lit	1
Eliot, George	Middlemarch * The Mill on the Floss * Silas Marner	Basic	English Lit	4
Eliot, T.S.	T.S. Eliot's Major Poets and Plays: "The Wasteland," "The Love Song of J. Alfred Prufrock," & Other Works	Basic	English Lit	6
Ellison, Ralph	The Invisible Man	Basic	American Lit	7
Emerson, Ralph Waldo	Emerson's Essays	Basic	American Lit	1
Euripides	Electra * Medea	Basic	Classics	1
Faulkner, William	Absalom, Absalom! * As I Lay Dying * The Bear * Go Down, Moses * Light in August	Basic	American Lit	4
	The Sound and the Fury * The Unvanquished	Basic	American Lit	5
	Absalom, Absalom! * As I Lay Dying * The Bear * Go Down, Moses * Light in August The Sound and the Fury * The Unvanquished	Authors	Faulkner	3
Fielding, Henry	Joseph Andrews	Basic	English Lit	1
	Tom Jones	Basic	English Lit	2
Fitzgerald, F. Scott	The Great Gatsby	Basic	American Lit	4
	Tender is the Night	Basic	American Lit	5
Flaubert, Gustave	Madame Bovary	Basic	European Lit	1
Forster, E.M.	A Passage to India	Basic	English Lit	6
Fowles, John	The French Lieutenant's Woman	Basic	English Lit	5
Frank, Anne	The Diary of Anne Frank	Basic	European Lit	2
Franklin, Benjamin	The Autobiography of Benjamin Franklin	Basic	American Lit	1
Gawain Poet	Sir Gawain and the Green Night	Basic	Classics	4
Goethe, Johann Wolfgang von	Faust - Parts I & II	Basic	European Lit	2
Golding, William	Lord of the Flies	Basic	English Lit	5
Greene, Graham	The Power and the Glory	Basic	English Lit	6
Griffin, John H.	Black Like Me	Basic	American Lit	6

AUTHOR	TITLE(S)	SERIES	LIBRARY	Vol
Haley, Alex	The Autobiography of Malcolm X	Basic	American Lit	6
see also Little, Malcolm				
Hardy, Thomas	Far from the Madding Crowd * Jude the Obscure * The Mayor of Casterbridge	Basic	English Lit	3
	The Return of the Native * Tess of the D'Urbervilles	Basic	English Lit	4
	Far from the Madding Crowd * Jude the Obscure * The Mayor of Casterbridge The Return of the Native * Tess of the D'Urbervilles	Authors	Hardy	4
Hawthorne, Nathaniel	The House of the Seven Gables* The Scarlet Letter	Basic	American Lit	1
Heller, Joseph	Catch-22	Basic	American Lit	6
Hemingway, Ernest	A Farewell to Arms * For Whom the Bell Tolls	Basic	American Lit	4
	The Old Man and the Sea	Basic	American Lit	7
	The Sun Also Rises	Basic	American Lit	5
	A Farewell to Arms * For Whom the Bell Tolls The Old Man and the Sea The Sun Also Rises	Authors	Hemingway	5
Herbert, Frank	Dune & Other Works	Basic	American Lit	6
Hesse, Herman	Demian * Steppenwolf & Siddhartha	Basic	European Lit	2
Hilton, James	Lost Horizon	Basic	English Lit	5
Homer	The Iliad * The Odyssey	Basic	Classics	1
Hugo, Victor	Les Miserables	Basic	European Lit	1
Huxley, Aldous	Brave New World & Brave New World Revisited	Basic	English Lit	5
Ibsen, Henrik	Ibsen's Plays I: A Doll's House & Hedda Gabler * Ibsen's Plays II: Ghosts, An Enemy of the People, & The Wild Duck	Basic	European Lit	4
James, Henry	The American * Daisy Miller & The Turn of the Screw * The Portrait of a Lady	Basic	American Lit	2
	The American * Daisy Miller & The Turn of the Screw * The Portrait of a Lady	Authors	James	6
Joyce, James	A Portrait of the Artist as a Young Man * Ulysses	Basic	English Lit	6
Kafka, Franz	Kafka's Short Stories * The Trial	Basic	European Lit	2
Keats & Shelley	Keats & Shelley	Basic	English Lit	1
Kesey, Ken	One Flew Over the Cuckoo's Nest	Basic	American Lit	7
Knowles, John	A Separate Peace	Basic	American Lit	7

AUTHOR	TITLE(S)	SERIES	LIBRARY	Vol
Lawrence, D.H.	Sons and Lovers	Basic	English Lit	6
Lee, Harper	To Kill a Mockingbird	Basic	American Lit	7
Lewis, Sinclair	Babbit * Main Street	Basic	American Lit	3
	Babbit * Main Street	Authors	Lewis	7
Little, Malcolm see also Haley, Alex	The Autobiography of Malcolm X	Basic	American Lit	6
London, Jack	Call of the Wild & White Fang	Basic	American Lit	3
Machiavelli, Niccolo	The Prince	Basic	Classics	4
Malamud, Bernard	The Assistant	Basic	American Lit	6
Malcolm X	see Little, Malcolm			
Malory, Thomas	Le Morte d'Arthur	Basic	Classics	4
Marlowe, Christopher	Doctor Faustus	Basic	Classics	3
Marquez, Gabriel Garcia	One Hundred Years of Solitude	Basic	American Lit	6
Maugham, Somerset	Of Human Bondage	Basic	English Lit	6
Melville, Herman	Billy Budd & Typee * Moby Dick	Basic	American Lit	1
Miller, Arthur	The Crucible * Death of a Salesman	Basic	American Lit	6
Milton, John	Paradise Lost	Basic	English Lit	2
Moliere, Jean Baptiste	Tartuffe, Misanthrope & Bourgeois Gentleman	Basic	European Lit	1
More, Thomas	Utopia	Basic	Classics	4
O'Connor, Flannery	O'Connor's Short Stories	Basic	American Lit	7
Orwell, George	Animal Farm	Basic	English Lit	5
	Nineteen Eighty-Four	Basic	English Lit	6
Paton, Alan	Cry, The Beloved Country	Basic	English Lit	5
Plath, Sylvia	The Bell Jar	Basic	American Lit	6
Plato	Plato's Euthyphro, Apology, Crito & Phaedo * Plato's The Republic	Basic	Classics	1
Poe, Edgar Allen	Poe's Short Stories	Basic	American Lit	1
Remarque, Erich	All Quiet on the Western Front	Basic	European Lit	2
Rolvaag, Ole	Giants in the Earth	Basic	European Lit	4
Rostand, Edmond	Cyrano de Bergerac	Basic	European Lit	1
Salinger, J.D.	The Catcher in the Rye	Basic	American Lit	6
Sartre, Jean Paul	No Exit & The Flies	Basic	European Lit	1
Scott, Walter	Ivanhoe	Basic	English Lit	1
Shaefer, Jack	Shane	Basic	American Lit	7
Shakespeare, William	All's Well that Ends Well & The Merry Wives of Windsor * As You Like It * The Comedy of Errors, Love's Labour's Lost, & The Two Gentlemen of Verona * Measure for Measure * The Merchant of Venice * Midsummer Night's Dream * Much Ado About Nothing * The Taming of the Shrew * The Tempest *	Basic	Shakespeare	1

AUTHOR	TITLE(S)	SERIES	LIBRARY	Vol
Shakespeare, William	Troilus and Cressida * Twelfth Night * The Winter's Tale	Basic	Shakespeare	1
	All's Well that Ends Well & The Merry Wives of Windsor * As You Like It * The Comedy of Errors, Love's Labour's Lost, & The Two Gentlemen of Verona * Measure for Measure * The Merchant of Venice * Midsummer Night's Dream * Much Ado About Nothing * The Taming of the Shrew * The Tempest * Troilus and Cressida * Twelfth Night * The Winter's Tale	Authors	Shakespeare	8
	Antony and Cleopatra * Hamlet * Julius Caesar * King Lear * Macbeth * Othello * Romeo and Juliet	Basic	Shakeapeare	2
	Antony and Cleopatra * Hamlet * Julius Caesar * King Lear * Macbeth * Othello * Romeo and Juliet	Authors	Shakespeare	9
	Henry IV Part 1 * Henry IV Part 2 * Henry V * Henry VI Parts 1,2,3 * Richard II * Richard III * Shakespeare's Sonnets	Basic	Shakespeare	3
	Henry IV Part 1 * Henry IV Part 2 * Henry V * Henry VI Parts 1,2,3 * Richard II * Richard III * Shakespeare's Sonnets	Authors	Shakespeare	10
Shaw, George Bernard	Man and Superman & Caesar and Cleopatra * Pygmalion & Arms and the Man	Basic	English Lit	6
	Man and Superman & Caesar and Cleopatra * Pygmalion & Arms and the Man	Authors	Shaw	11
Shelley, Mary	Frankenstein	Basic	English Lit	1
Sinclair, Upton	The Jungle	Basic	American Lit	3
Skinner, B.F.	Walden Two	Basic	American Lit	7
Solzhenitsyn, Aleksandr	One Day in the Life of Ivan Denisovich	Basic	European Lit	3
Sophocles	The Oedipus Trilogy	Basic	Classics	1
Spenser, Edmund	The Faerie Queen	Basic	Classics	4
Steinbeck, John	The Grapes of Wrath *	Basic	American Lit	4
	Of Mice and Men * The Pearl * The Red Pony	Basic	American Lit	5

AUTHOR INDEX

AUTHOR	TITLE(S)	SERIES	LIBRARY	Vol
Steinbeck, John	The Grapes of Wrath * Of Mice and Men * The Pearl * The Red Pony	Authors	Steinbeck	12
Stendhal	The Red and the Black	Basic	European Lit	1
Sterne, Lawrence	Tristram Shandy	Basic	English Lit	2
Stevenson, Robert Louis	Dr. Jekyll and Mr. Hyde *	Basic	English Lit	3
	Treasure Island & Kidnapped	Basic	English Lit	4
Stoker, Bram	Dracula	Basic	English Lit	3
Stowe, Harriet Beecher	Uncle Tom's Cabin	Basic	American Lit	2
Swift, Jonathan	Gulliver's Travels	Basic	English Lit	1
Thackeray, William Makepeace	Vanity Fair	Basic	English Lit	4
Thoreau, Henry David	Walden	Basic	American Lit	1
Tolkien, J.R.R.	The Lord of the Rings & The Hobbit	Basic	English Lit	5
Tolstoy, Leo	Anna Karenina * War and Peace	Basic	European Lit	3
Turgenev, Ivan Sergeyevich	Fathers and Sons	Basic	European Lit	3
Twain, Mark	A Connecticut Yankee * Huckleberry Finn * The Prince and the Pauper * Tom Sawyer	Basic	American Lit	2
	A Connecticut Yankee * Huckleberry Finn * The Prince and the Pauper * Tom Sawyer	Authors	Twain	13
Virgil	The Aeneid	Basic	Classics	1
Voltaire, Francois	Candide	Basic	European Lit	2
Vonnegut, Kurt	Vonnegut's Major Works	Basic	American Lit	7
Walker, Alice	The Color Purple	Basic	American Lit	7
Warren, Robert Penn	All the King's Men	Basic	American Lit	6
West, Nathanael	Miss Lonelyhearts & The Day of the Locust	Basic	American Lit	5
Wharton, Edith	Ethan Frome	Basic	American Lit	3
Whitman, Walt	Leaves of Grass	Basic	American Lit	1
Wilder, Thornton	Our Town	Basic	American Lit	5
Williams, Tennessee	The Glass Menagerie & A Streetcar Named Desire	Basic	American Lit	6
Woolf, Virginia	Mrs. Dalloway	Basic	English Lit	5
Wordsworth, William	The Prelude	Basic	English Lit	2
Wright, Richard	Black Boy	Basic	American Lit	4
	Native Son	Basic	American Lit	5

INDEX OF SERIES

<u>BASIC LIBRARY (24-0)</u>

THE SHAKESPEARE LIBRARY: 3 Volumes, 26 Titles (25-9)
- V. 1 - The Comedies 12 titles (00-3)
- V. 2 - The Tragedies, 7 titles (01-1)
- V. 3 - The Histories; The Sonnets, 7 titles (02-X)

THE CLASSICS LIBRARY: 4 Volumes, 27 Titles (26-7)
- V. 1 - Greek & Roman Classics, 11 titles (03-8)
- V. 2 - Greek & Roman Classics, 2 titles (04-6)
- V. 3 - Early Christian/European Classics, 7 titles (05-4)
- V. 4 - Early Christian/European Classics, 7 titles (06-2)

ENGLISH LITERATURE LIBRARY: 6 Volumes, 55 Titles (29-1)
- V. 1 - 17th Century & Romantic Period Classics, 7 titles (07-0)
- V. 2 - 17th Century & Romantic Period Classics, 7 titles (08-9)
- V. 3 - Victorian Age, 11 titles (09-7)
- V. 4 - Victorian Age, 10 titles (10-0)
- V. 5 - 20th Century, 10 titles (11-9)
- V. 6 - 20th Century, 10 titles (12-7)

AMERICAN LITERATURE LIBRARY: 7 Volumes, 77 Titles (33-X)
- V. 1 - Early U.S. & Romantic Period, 11 titles (13-5)
- V. 2 - Civil War to 1900, 11 titles (14-3)
- V. 3 - Early 20th Century, 9 titles (15-1)
- V. 4 - The Jazz Age to W.W.II, 11 titles (16-X)
- V. 5 - The Jazz Age to W.W.II, 10 titles (17-8)
- V. 6 - Post-War American Literature, 13 titles (18-6)
- V. 7 - Post-War American Literature, 12 titles (19-4)

EUROPEAN LITERATURE LIBRARY: 4 Volumes, 29 Titles (36-4)
- V. 1 - French Literature, 12 titles (20-8)
- V. 2 - German Literature, 7 titles (21-6)
- V. 3 - Russian Literature, 7 titles (22-4)
- V. 4 - Scandinavian Literature, 3 titles (23-2)

<u>AUTHORS LIBRARY (65-8)</u>

- V. 1 - **Charles Dickens** Library, 6 titles (66-6)
- V. 2 - **Feodor Dostoevsky** Library, 3 titles (67-4)
- V. 3 - **William Faulkner** Library, 7 titles (68-2)
- V. 4 - **Thomas Hardy** Library, 5 titles (69-0)
- V. 5 - **Ernest Hemingway** Library, 4 titles (70-4)
- V. 6 - **Henry James** Library, 3 titles (71-2)
- V. 7 - **Sinclair Lewis** Library, 2 titles (72-0)
- V. 8 - **Shakespeare** Library, Part 1 - The Comedies, 12 titles (73-9)
- V. 9 - **Shakespeare** Library, Part 2 - The Tragedies, 7 titles (74-7)
- V. 10 - **Shakespeare** Library, Part 3 - The Histories; Sonnets, 7 titles (75-5)
- V. 11 - **George Bernard Shaw** Library, 2 titles (76-3)
- V. 12 - **John Steinbeck** Library, 4 titles (77-1)
- V. 13 - **Mark Twain** Library, 4 titles (78-X)

Moonbeam Publications ISBN Prefix: 0-931013-

HARDBOUND LITERARY LIBRARIES

INDEX OF LIBRARIES

This is the INDEX OF LIBRARIES, listing the volumes and the individual titles within the volumes for both the BASIC LIBRARY SERIES (24 Volumes, starting below) and the AUTHORS LIBRARY SERIES (13 Volumes, see Page 6).

BASIC LIBRARY SERIES (24 Volumes)

THE SHAKESPEARE LIBRARY: 3 Volumes, 26 Titles

Vol 1 - The Comedies (12 titles)
All's Well that Ends Well & The Merry Wives of Windsor * As You Like It * The Comedy of Errors, Love's Labour's Lost, & The Two Gentlemen of Verona * Measure for Measure * The Merchant of Venice * A Midsummer Night's Dream * Much Ado About Nothing * The Taming of the Shrew * The Tempest * Troilus and Cressida * Twelfth Night * The Winter's Tale

Vol 2 - The Tragedies (7 titles)
Antony and Cleopatra * Hamlet * Julius Caesar * King Lear * Macbeth * Othello * Romeo and Juliet

Vol 3 - The Histories; The Sonnets (7 titles)
Henry IV Part 1 * Henry IV Part 2 * Henry V * Henry VI Parts 1,2,3 * Richard II * Richard III * Shakespeare's Sonnets

THE CLASSICS LIBRARY: 4 Volumes, 27 Titles

Vol 1 - Greek & Roman Classics Part 1 (11 titles)
The Aeneid * Agamemnon * Aristotle's Ethics * Euripides' Electra & Medea * The Iliad * Lysistrata & Other Comedies * Mythology * The Odyssey * Oedipus Trilogy * Plato's Euthyphro, Apology, Crito & Phaedo * Plato's The Republic

THE CLASSICS LIBRARY (cont'd)

Vol 2 - Greek & Roman Classics Part 2 (2 titles)
*Greek Classics * Roman Classics*

Vol 3 - Early Christian/European Classics Part 1 (7 titles)
*Beowulf * Canterbury Tales * Divine Comedy - I. Inferno * Divine Comedy - II. Purgatorio * Divine Comedy - III. Paradiso * Doctor Faustus * Don Quixote*

Vol 4 - Early Christian/European Classics Part 2 (7 titles)
*The Faerie Queene * Le Morte D'Arthur * New Testament * Old Testament * The Prince * Sir Gawain and the Green Knight * Utopia*

ENGLISH LITERATURE LIBRARY: 6 Volumes, 55 Titles

Vol 1 - 17th Century & Romantic Period Classics Part 1 (7 titles)
*Emma * Frankenstein * Gulliver's Travels * Ivanhoe * Joseph Andrews * Keats & Shelley * Moll Flanders*

Vol 2 - 17th Century & Romantic Period Classics Part 2 (7 titles)
*Paradise Lost * Pilgrim's Progress * The Prelude * Pride and Prejudice * Robinson Crusoe * Tom Jones * Tristram Shandy*

Vol 3 - Victorian Age Part 1 (11 titles)
*Alice in Wonderland * Bleak House * David Copperfield * Dr. Jekyll and Mr. Hyde * Dracula * Far from the Madding Crowd * Great Expectations * Hard Times * Jane Eyre * Jude the Obscure * The Mayor of Casterbridge*

ENGLISH LITERATURE LIBRARY (cont'd)

Vol 4 - Victorian Age Part 2 (10 titles)
*Middlemarch * The Mill on the Floss * Oliver Twist * The Return of the Native * Silas Marner * A Tale of Two Cities * Tess of the D'Urbervilles * Treasure Island & Kidnapped * Vanity Fair * Wuthering Heights*

Vol 5 - 20th Century Part 1 (10 titles)
*Animal Farm * Brave New World * Cry, The Beloved Country * The French Lieutenant's Woman * Heart of Darkness & The Secret Sharer * Lord Jim * Lord of the Flies * The Lord of the Rings * Lost Horizon * Mrs. Dalloway*

Vol 6 - 20th Century Part 2 (10 titles)
*Nineteen Eighty-Four * Of Human Bondage * A Passage to India * A Portrait of the Artist as a Young Man * The Power and the Glory * Shaw's Man and Superman & Caesar and Cleopatra * Shaw's Pygmalion & Arms and the Man * Sons and Lovers * T.S. Eliot's Major Poems and Plays * Ulysses*

AMERICAN LITERATURE LIBRARY: 7 Volumes, 77 Titles

Vol 1 - Early U.S. & Romantic Period (11 titles)
*Autobiography of Ben Franklin * Billy Budd & Typee * The Deerslayer * Emerson's Essays * The House of Seven Gables * The Last of the Mohicans * Leaves of Grass * Moby Dick * Poe's Short Stories * The Scarlet Letter * Walden*

AMERICAN LITERATURE LIBRARY (cont'd)

Vol 2 - Civil War to 1900 (11 titles)
*The American * The Awakening * A Connecticut Yankee in King Arthur's Court * Daisy Miller & The Turn of the Screw * Emily Dickinson: Selected Poems * Huckleberry Finn * The Portrait of a Lady * The Prince and the Pauper * Red Badge of Courage * Tom Sawyer * Uncle Tom's Cabin*

Vol 3 - Early 20th Century (9 titles)
*An American Tragedy * Babbitt * Call of the Wild & White Fang * Ethan Frome * The Jungle * Main Street * My Antonia * Sister Carrie * Winesburg, Ohio*

Vol 4 - The Jazz Age to W.W.II Part 1 (11 titles)
*Absalom, Absalom! * As I Lay Dying * The Bear * Black Boy * A Farewell to Arms * For Whom the Bell Tolls * Go Down, Moses * The Good Earth * The Grapes of Wrath * The Great Gatsby * Light in August*

Vol 5 - The Jazz Age to W.W.II Part 2 (10 titles)
*Miss Lonelyhearts & The Day of the Locust * Native Son * Of Mice and Men * Our Town * The Pearl * The Red Pony * The Sound and the Fury * The Sun Also Rises * Tender is the Night * Unvanquished*

Vol 6 - Post-War American Literature Part 1 (13 titles)
*100 Years of Solitude * All the King's Men * The Assistant * The Autobiography of Malcolm X * The Bell Jar * Black Like Me * Catch-22 * The Catcher in the Rye * The Color Purple * The Crucible * Death of a Salesman * Dune and Other Works * The Glass Menagerie & A Streetcar Named Desire*

AMERICAN LITERATURE LIBRARY (cont'd)

Vol 7 - Post-War American Literature Part 2 (12 titles)
*The Invisible Man * Manchild in the Promised Land * O'Connor's Short Stories * The Old Man and the Sea * One Flew Over the Cuckoo's Nest * The Ox-Bow Incident * A Separate Peace * Shane * To Kill a Mockingbird * Vonnegut's Major Works * Walden Two * Who's Afraid of Virginia Woolf?*

EUROPEAN LITERATURE LIBRARY: 4 Volumes, 29 Titles

Vol 1 - French Literature (12 titles)
*Candide * The Count of Monte Cristo * Cyrano de Bergerac * Les Miserables * Madame Bovary * No Exit & The Flies * The Plague * The Red and the Black * The Stranger * Tartuffe, Misanthrope & Bourgeois Gentlemen * The Three Musketeers * Waiting for Godot*

Vol 2 - German Literature (7 titles)
*All Quiet on the Western Front * Demian * The Diary of Anne Frank * Faust Pt. I & Pt. II * Kafka's Short Stories * Steppenwolf & Siddhartha * The Trial*

Vol 3 - Russian Literature (7 titles)
*Anna Karenina * The Brothers Karamozov * Crime and Punishment * Fathers and Sons * Notes from the Underground * One Day in the Life of Ivan Denisovich * War and Peace*

Vol 4 - Scandinavian Literature (3 titles)
*Giants in the Earth * Ibsen's Plays I: A Doll's House & Hedda Gabler * Ibsen's Plays II: Ghosts, An Enemy of the People & The Wild Duck*

AUTHORS LIBRARY

Vol 1 -Charles Dickens Library (6 titles)
*Bleak House * David Copperfield * Great Expectations *
Hard Times * Oliver Twist * A Tale of Two Cities*

Vol 2 - Feodor Dostoevsky Library (3 titles)
*The Brothers Karamazov * Crime and Punishment *
Notes from the Underground*

Vol 3 - William Faulkner Library (7 titles)
*Absalom, Absalom! * As I Lay Dying * The Bear * Go
Down, Moses * Light in August * The Sound and the Fury
* The Unvanquished*

Vol 4 - Thomas Hardy Library (5 titles)
*Far from the Madding Crowd * Jude the Obscure * The
Major of Casterbridge * The Return of the Native * Tess
of the D'Urbervilles*

Vol 5 - Ernest Hemingway Library (4 titles)
*A Farewell to Arms * For Whom the Bell Tolls * The Old
Man and the Sea * The Sun Also Rises*

Vol 6 - Henry James Library (3 titles)
*The American * Daisy Miller & The Turn of the Screw *
The Portrait of a Lady*

Vol 7 - Sinclair Lewis Library (2 titles)
*Babbitt * Main Street*

Vol 8 - Shakespeare Library, Part 1 - The Comedies (12 titles)
*All's Well that Ends Well & The Merry Wives of Windsor
* As You Like It * The Comedy of Errors, Love's Labour's
Lost & The Two Gentlemen of Verona * Measure for
Measure * The Merchant of Venice * A Midsummer
Night's Dream * Much Ado About Nothing * The Taming
of the Shrew * The Tempest * Troilus and Cressida *
Twelfth Night * The Winter's Tale*

Vol 9 - Shakespeare Library, Part 2 - The Tragedies (7 Titles)
*Antony and Cleopatra * Hamlet * Julius Caesar * King
Lear * Macbeth * Othello * Romeo and Juliet*

**Vol 10 - Shakespeare Library, Part 3 - The Histories; The
Sonnets (7 titles)**
*Henry IV Part 1 * Henry IV Part 2 * Henry V * Henry VI
Parts 1,2,3 * Richard II * Richard III * Shakespeare's The
Sonnets*

Vol 11 - George Bernard Shaw Library (2 titles)
*Pygmalion & Arms and the Man * Man and Superman &
Caesar and Cleopatra*

Vol 12 - John Steinbeck Library (4 titles)
*The Grapes of Wrath * Of Mice and Men * The Pearl *
The Red Pony*

Vol 13 - Mark Twain Library (4 titles)
*A Connecticut Yankee in King Arthur's Court * Huckle-
berry Finn * The Prince and the Pauper * Tom Sawyer*